# Monitoring Elasticsearch

Monitor your Elasticsearch cluster's health, and diagnose and solve its performance and reliability issues

**Dan Noble**

**[PACKT] open source \***
PUBLISHING   community experience distilled

BIRMINGHAM - MUMBAI

# Monitoring Elasticsearch

First published: July 2016

Production reference: 1200716

Published by Packt Publishing Ltd.
Livery Place
35 Livery Street
Birmingham B3 2PB, UK.

ISBN 978-1-78439-780-7

www.packtpub.com

# Credits

**Author**
Dan Noble

**Reviewers**
James A. Cubeta
Joseph E McMahon
Parkhe Kishor B.

**Acquisition Editor**
Sonali Vernekar

**Content Development Editors**
Amey Varangaonkar
Merint Mathew

**Technical Editor**
Hussain Kanchwala

**Copy Editor**
Priyanka Ravi

**Project Coordinator**
Judie Jose

**Proofreader**
Safis Editing

**Indexer**
Rekha Nair

**Graphics**
Kirk D'Penha

**Production Coordinator**
Melwyn Dsa

**Cover Work**
Melwyn Dsa

# About the Author

**Dan Noble** is a software engineer with a passion for writing secure, clean, and articulate code. He enjoys working with a variety of programming languages and software frameworks, particularly Python, Elasticsearch, and frontend technologies. Dan currently works on geospatial web applications and data processing systems.

Dan has been a user and advocate of Elasticsearch since 2011. He has given talks about Elasticsearch at various meetup groups, and is the author of the Python Elasticsearch client **rawes**. Dan was also a technical reviewer for the *Elasticsearch Cookbook*, *Second Edition*, by Alberto Paro.

I would like to thank my beautiful wife, Julie, for putting up with me while I wrote this book. Thanks for supporting me every step of the way.

I would also like to thank my friends and colleagues James Cubeta, Joe McMahon, and Mahmoud Lababidi, who shared their insight, time, and support. I would like to give a special thanks to Abe Usher – you have been an incredible mentor over the years.

Finally, thanks to everyone at Packt Publishing for helping to make this book happen. A special thanks to Merint Mathew, Sonali Vernekar, Hussain Kanchwala, and Amey Varangaonkar for your valuable and careful feedback.

# About the Reviewers

**James A. Cubeta** is a computer scientist with more than 20 years of experience, spanning government contracting, commercial companies, and research organizations. With a technical emphasis on data management, ETL, multi-tier application development, and relational and NoSQL databases, he has also helped author Java courses at Sun Microsystems and served as a technical reviewer for O'Reilly Media's extremely successful book *Head First Java*. He is currently a senior technologist at the HumanGeo Group, LLC.

**Joseph E McMahon** is a computer scientist with over 25 years of experience developing distributed systems with a focus on effective and performant messaging components. He has vast experience integrating geospatial solutions and data collection architectures. Currently, he leads a division in The HumanGeo Group supporting a variety of government customers. When not coding, he enjoys cooking, woodworking, and traveling with his wife and three children.

**Parkhe Kishor B.** received a BSc degree and an MTech degree in industrial mathematics and computer applications from the University of Pune. He joined High Mark Credit Information Service in 2012, where he worked as senior software engineer in the research and development department. He also has experience working in information retrieval, big data, and distributed computing. He is currently working as a design engineer at Introp Software Solutions, India. He is frequently a consultant to the industry in the area of big data, NoSQL, machine learning, artificial intelligence, and business intelligence.

# www.PacktPub.com

## eBooks, discount offers, and more

Did you know that Packt offers eBook versions of every book published, with PDF and ePub files available? You can upgrade to the eBook version at www.PacktPub.com and as a print book customer, you are entitled to a discount on the eBook copy. Get in touch with us at customercare@packtpub.com for more details.

At www.PacktPub.com, you can also read a collection of free technical articles, sign up for a range of free newsletters and receive exclusive discounts and offers on Packt books and eBooks.

https://www2.packtpub.com/books/subscription/packtlib

Do you need instant solutions to your IT questions? PacktLib is Packt's online digital book library. Here, you can search, access, and read Packt's entire library of books.

## Why subscribe?

- Fully searchable across every book published by Packt
- Copy and paste, print, and bookmark content
- On demand and accessible via a web browser

# Table of Contents

**Preface**                                                                      **v**

**Chapter 1: Introduction to Monitoring Elasticsearch**                           **1**

  **An overview of Elasticsearch**                                      **1**

    Learning more about Elasticsearch                          1

    Data distribution, redundancy, and fault tolerance         2

    Full-text search                                           5

    Similar technologies                                       7

      Apache Lucene                                    7

      Solr                                             8

      Ferret                                           8

  **Monitoring Elasticsearch**                                          **8**

  **Resourcefulness and problem solving**                               **9**

  **Summary**                                                          **10**

**Chapter 2: Installation and the Requirements for Elasticsearch**               **11**

  **Installing Elasticsearch**                                         **12**

    DEB/RPM installation                                       13

    The yum and apt-get repositories                           13

    Ubuntu/Debian and apt-get                                  13

    CentOS/RHEL and yum                                        14

    Verification                                               14

    Configuration files                                        16

  **Configuring an Elasticsearch cluster**                             **16**

    Cluster name                                               16

    Memory configuration                                       17

    Open file limit                                            17

    The maximum file limit                                     17

Updating max file descriptors on Ubuntu Linux 18
Enabling pluggable authentication modules 19
Verifying the open file limit 19
Disabling swapping 20
**Understanding your cluster** **21**
Installing Elasticsearch-head 21
Installing Bigdesk 23
Marvel 24
**Cluster requirements** **26**
**Summary** **27**
**Chapter 3: Elasticsearch-head and Bigdesk** **29**
**Cluster setup** **29**
Cluster configuration 30
Sample data 31
**Elasticsearch-head** **33**
The Overview tab 33
Cluster states 34
Node and index actions 37
The Indices tab 39
The Browser tab 40
The Structured Query tab 40
The Any Request tab 41
The official website 42
**Bigdesk** **42**
**The Elasticsearch cat API** **46**
Background 46
Count 47
Health 47
Indices 48
Shards 49
**Summary** **49**
**Chapter 4: Marvel Dashboard** **51**
**Setting up Marvel** **51**
**Upgrading Marvel** **56**
**Configuring Marvel** **57**
Marvel agent configuration settings 58
**Marvel index configuration** **59**
**Understanding the Marvel dashboard** **61**
Overview dashboard 63
Indices dashboard 66

Nodes dashboard                                                        69
**Monitoring node failures**                                           **71**
**Summary**                                                            **72**
**Chapter 5: System Monitoring**                                       **73**
  **Working with Kopf**                                                **73**
    Installing Kopf                                                    74
      The cluster page                                                 76
      The nodes page                                                   77
      The rest page                                                    78
      The more dropdown                                                79
  **Working with Logstash and Kibana**                                 **80**
    ELK                                                                80
    Installation                                                       80
      Installing Logstash                                              81
      Loading NGINX logs                                               81
      Installing Kibana                                                84
  **Working with Nagios**                                              **92**
    Installing Nagios                                                  92
  **Command line tools for system and process management**             **97**
    top                                                                97
    tail                                                               98
    grep                                                               98
    ps                                                                 99
    kill                                                               100
    free                                                               101
    du and df                                                          101
  **Summary**                                                          **102**
**Chapter 6: Troubleshooting Performance and Reliability**
**Issues**                                                             **105**
  **System configuration**                                            **105**
  **The fielddata cache**                                             **106**
  **Analyzing queries**                                               **108**
    Slow log                                                           108
  **Improving query performance**                                     **110**
    High-cardinality fields                                            110
    Querying smaller indices                                           110
    Cold indices                                                       111
    The shard query cache                                              115
    Script queries                                                     117
    Testing meticulously                                               117

**System and data architecting** **118**

Hot-Warm architecture 118

Master nodes 118

Hot nodes 118

Warm nodes 118

Reducing disk size 119

Compression 119

Storing the _source and analyzed fields 120

Optimizing data ingestion 121

Bulk indexing operations 122

Drive configuration 124

**Case studies** **124**

Node configuration 124

Query optimization 126

Web application performance 129

**Summary** **130**

**Chapter 7: Node Failure and Post-Mortem Analysis** **131**

**Diagnosing problems** **131**

OutOfMemoryError exceptions 132

Shard failures 133

Slow queries 137

Resolving OutOfMemoryError exceptions 138

Elasticsearch process crashes 141

Disk space 142

Resolving the issue 143

**Reviewing some case studies** **143**

The ES process quits unexpectedly 144

Query requests slow and timing out 145

**Summary** **146**

**Chapter 8: Looking Forward** **147**

**Elasticsearch 5 overview** **147**

Performance and reliability 148

Data loss 149

**Upgrading to Elasticsearch 5.0** **149**

When to upgrade 152

**Monitoring Elasticsearch 5** **153**

**Summary** **154**

**Index** **157**

# Preface

Welcome to *Monitoring Elasticsearch*!

There are many books and online tutorials that cover the Elasticsearch API and how to configure a cluster. But, until now, there hasn't been a thorough, accessible resource for monitoring and troubleshooting purposes. We've found that Elasticsearch monitoring tools drastically improve our ability to solve cluster issues and greatly increase cluster reliability and performance as a result. We wrote this book to share those use cases and the insights that came out of them.

This book covers how to use several popular open source and commercial Elasticsearch monitoring tools, namely, Elasticsearch-head, Bigdesk, Marvel, Kopf, and Kibana. There's also a section on the Elasticsearch cat API and how to use Nagios to perform general system monitoring. Moreover, we will discuss several case studies with real-world examples of troubleshooting Elasticsearch issues using these tools.

We believe that the best way to learn is to do. In this book, we'll go over how to set up a sample Elasticsearch cluster and load it with data. At times, we'll deliberately introduce problems into the cluster so that we can see how the errors are tracked using our various monitoring tools. Following along with these examples in your own cluster will help you learn both how to use the monitoring tools and how to tackle new and unknown issues that may arise.

After reading this book, we hope that you will be better equipped to run and maintain an Elasticsearch cluster. You will also be more prepared to diagnose and solve cluster issues, such as a node going down, the Elasticsearch process dying, configuration errors, shard errors, `OutOfMemoryError` exceptions, slow queries, and slow indexing performance.

# What this book covers

*Chapter 1, Introduction to Monitoring Elasticsearch,* gives an overview of Elasticsearch and talks about some things to keep in mind when monitoring a cluster or troubleshooting a problem.

*Chapter 2, Installation and the Requirements for Elasticsearch,* covers how to install Elasticsearch and several Elasticsearch monitoring tools.

*Chapter 3, Elasticsearch-head and Bigdesk,* demonstrates how to configure a multinode Elasticsearch cluster and how to use the monitoring tools Elasticsearch-head and Bigdesk to examine the health and status of a cluster.

*Chapter 4, Marvel Dashboard,* goes over Marvel, a commercial monitoring tool created by the makers of Elasticsearch.

*Chapter 5, System Monitoring,* covers the Elasticsearch utilities Kopf, Kibana, the Elasticsearch cat API, and several Unix command-line utilities. This chapter also demonstrates how to use Nagios for general system monitoring.

*Chapter 6, Troubleshooting Performance and Reliability Issues,* covers how to tackle some of the common performance and reliability issues that arise when using Elasticsearch. It also contains case studies with some real-world examples of troubleshooting.

*Chapter 7, Node Failure and Post-Mortem Analysis,* dives into analyzing your cluster's historical performance and how to get to the bottom of and recover from system failures. It also contains some case studies with real-world examples.

*Chapter 8, Looking Forward,* concludes the book by discussing what is to come with Elasticsearch 5, the next major software release, and some new monitoring tools that will be available for the release.

# What you need for this book

To follow along with the examples in this book, you'll need a real or virtualized three-node Elasticsearch cluster. You may optionally want two other nodes to run Marvel and Nagios, covered in *Chapter 4, Marvel Dashboard,* and *Chapter 5, System Monitoring,* respectively. It is possible to run Marvel and Nagios on the same host as a node in your Elasticsearch cluster, but you shouldn't do this in a production cluster. Check out VMWare Player (`https://www.vmware.com/products/player`) and VirtualBox (`https://www.virtualbox.org/wiki/Downloads`) for standing up your own virtual five-node environment or Amazon EC2 (`https://aws.amazon.com/ec2/`) for building a cluster in the cloud.

For your Elasticsearch nodes, you'll need a 64-bit version of Windows, Mac OS X, or Linux and a recent distribution of the Java Runtime Environment. The CPU speed doesn't matter as much on these hosts, but we recommend that you have at least 512 MB of memory per node. We use Ubuntu 14.04 and Oracle Java 7 for all examples in this book, but any modern operating system and either OpenJDK or Oracle Java 7 and 8 will work for running through the examples. The only exception is Nagios, which needs to run on Linux.

You will need the following software packages:

- Java 7 or Java 8 (`http://www.oracle.com/technetwork/java/javase/downloads/index.html`)
- Elasticsearch 2.3.2 (`https://www.elastic.co/downloads/past-releases/elasticsearch-2-3-2`)
- Elasticsearch-head (`https://github.com/mobz/elasticsearch-head`)
- Bigdesk (`http://bigdesk.org/`)
- Marvel — free for development, subscription fee for use in production (`https://www.elastic.co/downloads/marvel`)
- Kibana (`https://www.elastic.co/downloads/kibana`)
- Kopf (`https://github.com/lmenezes/elasticsearch-kopf`)
- Nagios (`https://www.nagios.org/downloads/`)

All of these software packages are free and open source except for Marvel, which is only free for use in development.

Finally, several examples in this book use the `curl` (`https://curl.haxx.se/`) command-line utility for making REST calls to Elasticsearch and, optionally, Python 2.7 for pretty-printing the results.

# Who this book is for

This book is for software developers, DevOps engineers, and system administrators who use Elasticsearch. We'll cover the basics of Elasticsearch to get a simple cluster installed and configured, but we will avoid going into detail about the Elasticsearch API. Thus, a basic understanding of the Elasticsearch API may be helpful, though not required, to understand this book.

# Conventions

In this book, you will find a number of text styles that distinguish between different kinds of information. Here are some examples of these styles and an explanation of their meaning.

Code words in text, database table names, folder names, filenames, file extensions, pathnames, dummy URLs, user input, and Twitter handles are shown as follows: "Now we'll install Marvel on the `elasticsearch-marvel-01`."

A block of code is set as follows:

```
cluster.name: my_elasticsearch_cluster
node.name: "elasticsearch-node-01"
discovery.zen.ping.multicast.enabled: false
discovery.zen.ping.unicast.hosts: ["elasticsearch-node-02",
  "elasticsearch-node-03"]
```

When we wish to draw your attention to a particular part of a code block, the relevant lines or items are set in bold:

```
cluster.name: my_elasticsearch_cluster
node.name: "elasticsearch-node-01"
discovery.zen.ping.multicast.enabled: false
discovery.zen.ping.unicast.hosts: ["elasticsearch-node-02",
  "elasticsearch-node-03"]
```

Any command-line input or output is written as follows:

```
# sudo service elasticsearch start
```

**New terms** and **important words** are shown in bold. Words that you see on the screen, for example, in menus or dialog boxes, appear in the text like this: "Clicking the **Next** button moves you to the next screen."

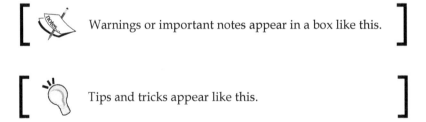

Warnings or important notes appear in a box like this.

Tips and tricks appear like this.

# Reader feedback

Feedback from our readers is always welcome. Let us know what you think about this book—what you liked or disliked. Reader feedback is important for us as it helps us develop titles that you will really get the most out of.

To send us general feedback, simply e-mail feedback@packtpub.com, and mention the book's title in the subject of your message.

If there is a topic that you have expertise in and you are interested in either writing or contributing to a book, see our author guide at www.packtpub.com/authors.

# Customer support

Now that you are the proud owner of a Packt book, we have a number of things to help you to get the most from your purchase.

# Downloading the example code

You can download the example code files for this book from your account at http://www.packtpub.com. If you purchased this book elsewhere, you can visit http://www.packtpub.com/support and register to have the files e-mailed directly to you.

You can download the code files by following these steps:

1. Log in or register to our website using your e-mail address and password.
2. Hover the mouse pointer on the **SUPPORT** tab at the top.
3. Click on **Code Downloads & Errata**.
4. Enter the name of the book in the **Search** box.
5. Select the book for which you're looking to download the code files.
6. Choose from the drop-down menu where you purchased this book from.
7. Click on **Code Download**.

You can also download the code files by clicking on the **Code Files** button on the book's webpage at the Packt Publishing website. This page can be accessed by entering the book's name in the **Search** box. Please note that you need to be logged in to your Packt account.

Once the file is downloaded, please make sure that you unzip or extract the folder using the latest version of:

- WinRAR / 7-Zip for Windows
- Zipeg / iZip / UnRarX for Mac
- 7-Zip / PeaZip for Linux

The code bundle for the book is also hosted on GitHub at `https://github.com/ PacktPublishing/Monitoring-Elasticsearch`. We also have other code bundles from our rich catalog of books and videos available at `https://github.com/ PacktPublishing/`. Check them out!

# Downloading the color images of this book

We also provide you with a PDF file that has color images of the screenshots/diagrams used in this book. The color images will help you better understand the changes in the output. You can download this file from `https://www.packtpub.com/sites/ default/files/downloads/MonitoringElasticsearch_ColorImages.pdf`.

# Errata

Although we have taken every care to ensure the accuracy of our content, mistakes do happen. If you find a mistake in one of our books—maybe a mistake in the text or the code—we would be grateful if you could report this to us. By doing so, you can save other readers from frustration and help us improve subsequent versions of this book. If you find any errata, please report them by visiting `http://www.packtpub. com/submit-errata`, selecting your book, clicking on the **Errata Submission Form** link, and entering the details of your errata. Once your errata are verified, your submission will be accepted and the errata will be uploaded to our website or added to any list of existing errata under the Errata section of that title.

To view the previously submitted errata, go to `https://www.packtpub.com/books/ content/support` and enter the name of the book in the search field. The required information will appear under the **Errata** section.

# Piracy

Piracy of copyrighted material on the Internet is an ongoing problem across all media. At Packt, we take the protection of our copyright and licenses very seriously. If you come across any illegal copies of our works in any form on the Internet, please provide us with the location address or website name immediately so that we can pursue a remedy.

Please contact us at copyright@packtpub.com with a link to the suspected pirated material.

We appreciate your help in protecting our authors and our ability to bring you valuable content.

# Questions

If you have a problem with any aspect of this book, you can contact us at questions@packtpub.com, and we will do our best to address the problem.

# 1
# Introduction to Monitoring Elasticsearch

Elasticsearch is a distributed and horizontally scalable full-text search engine with built-in data redundancy. It is a powerful and incredibly useful tool. However, as with any distributed system, problems may arise as it scales with more nodes and more data.

The information provided by Elasticsearch monitoring tools can drastically improve your ability to solve cluster issues and greatly increase cluster reliability and performance as a result. This chapter gives an overview of Elasticsearch and talks about why and how to monitor a cluster.

Specifically, this chapter covers the following topics:

- An overview of Elasticsearch
- Monitoring Elasticsearch
- Resourcefulness and problem solving

## An overview of Elasticsearch

This section gives a high-level overview of Elasticsearch and discusses some related full-text search products.

## Learning more about Elasticsearch

Elasticsearch is a free and open source full-text search engine that is built on top of Apache Lucene. Out of the box, Elasticsearch supports horizontal scaling and data redundancy. Released in 2010, Elasticsearch quickly gained recognition in the full-text search space. Its scalability features helped the tool gain market share against similar technologies such as Apache Solr.

Elasticsearch is a persistent document store and retrieval system, and it is similar to a database. However, it is different from relational databases such as MySQL, PostgreSQL, and Oracle in many ways:

- **Distributed**: Elasticsearch stores data and executes queries across multiple data nodes. This improves scalability, reliability, and performance.

- **Fault tolerant**: Data is replicated across multiple nodes in an Elasticsearch cluster, so if one node goes down, data is still available.

- **Full-text search**: Elasticsearch is built on top of Lucene, a full-text search technology, allowing it to understand and search natural language text.

- **JSON document store**: Elasticsearch stores documents as JSON instead of as rows in a table.

- **NoSQL**: Elasticsearch uses a JSON-based query language as opposed to a sequel query language (SQL).

- **Non-relational**: Unlike relational databases, Elasticsearch doesn't support *JOINS* across tables.

- **Analytics**: Elasticsearch has built-in analytical capabilities, such as word aggregations, geospatial queries, and scripting language support.

- **Dynamic Mappings**: A *mapping* in Elasticsearch is analogous to a *schema* in the relational database world. If the data type for a document field isn't explicitly defined, Elasticsearch will dynamically assign a type to it.

# Data distribution, redundancy, and fault tolerance

*Figures 1.1* through *1.4* explain how Elasticsearch distributes data across multiple nodes and how it automatically recovers from node failures:

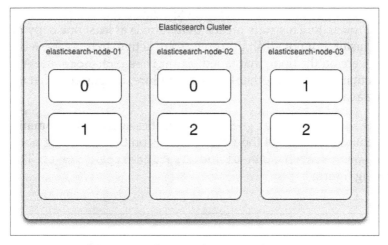

Figure 1.1: Elasticsearch Data Distribution

In this figure, we have an Elasticsearch cluster made up of three nodes: `elasticsearch-node-01`, `elasticsearch-node-02`, and `elasticsearch-node-03`. Our data index, is broken into three pieces, called **shards**. These shards are labeled `0`, `1`, and `2`. Each shard is replicated once; this means that there is a redundant copy of all shards. The cluster is colored green because the cluster is in good health; all data shards and replicas are available.

Let's say that the `elasticsearch-node-03` host experiences a hardware failure and shuts down. The following figures show what happens to the cluster in this scenario:

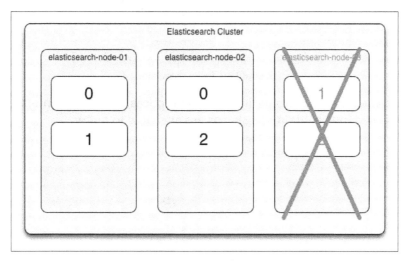

Figure 1.2: Node failure

*Figure 1.2* shows elasticsearch-node-03 experiencing a failure, and the cluster entering a yellow state. This state means that there is at least one copy of each shard active in the cluster, but not all shard replicas are active. In our case, a copy of the 1 and 2 shards were on the node that failed, elasticsearch-node-03. A yellow state also warns us that if there's another hardware failure, it's possible that not all data shards will be available.

When elasticsearch-node-03 goes down, Elasticsearch will automatically start rebuilding redundant copies of the 1 and 2 shards on the remaining nodes; in our case, this is elasticsearch-node-01 and elasticsearch-node-02. This is shown in the following figure:

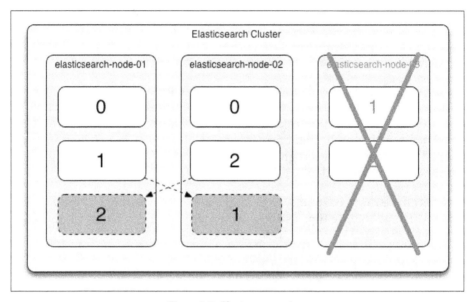

Figure 1.3: Cluster recovering

Once Elasticsearch finishes rebuilding the data replicas, the cluster enters a green state once again. Now, all data and shards are available to query.

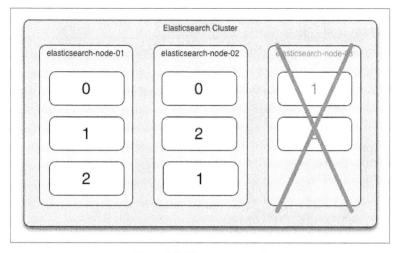

Figure 1.4: Cluster recovered

The cluster recovery process demonstrated in *Figures 1.3* and *1.4* happens automatically in Elasticsearch. No extra configuration or user action is required.

# Full-text search

**Full-text** search refers to running keyword queries against natural-language text documents. A document can be something, such as a newspaper article, a blog post, a forum post, or a tweet. In fact, many popular newspapers, forums, and social media websites, such as The New York Times, Stack Overflow, and Foursquare, use Elasticsearch.

Assume that we were to store the following text string in Elasticsearch:

```
We demand rigidly defined areas of doubt and uncertainty!
```

A user can find this document by searching Elasticsearch using keywords, such as *demand* or *doubt*. Elasticsearch also supports word stemming. This means that if we searched for the word *define*, Elasticsearch would still find this document because the root word of *defined* is *define*.

This piece of text, along with some additional metadata, may be stored as follows in Elasticsearch in the JSON format:

```
{
    "text" : "We demand rigidly defined areas of doubt and
uncertainty!",
    "author" : "Douglas Adams",
    "published" : "1979-10-12",
```

```
        "likes" : 583,
        "source" : "The Hitchhiker's Guide to the Galaxy",
        "tags" : ["science fiction", "satire"]
}
```

If we let Elasticsearch dynamically assign a mapping (think *schema*) to this document, it would look like this:

```
{
    "quote" : {
        "properties" : {
            "author" : {
                "type" : "string"
            },
            "likes" : {
                "type" : "long"
            },
            "published" : {
                "type" : "date",
                "format" : "strict_date_optional_time||epoch_millis"
            },
            "source" : {
                "type" : "string"
            },
            "tags" : {
                "type" : "string"
            },
            "text" : {
                "type" : "string"
            }
        }
    }
}
```

Note that Elasticsearch was able to pick up that the `published` field looked like a date.

An Elasticsearch query that searches for this document looks like this:

```
{
    "query" : {
        "query_string" : {
            "query" : "demand rigidly"
        }
    },
    "size" : 10
}
```

Specifics about Elasticsearch mappings and the Search API are beyond the scope of this book, but you can learn more about them through the official Elasticsearch documentation at the following links:

- **Elasticsearch Mappings**: https://www.elastic.co/guide/en/
  elasticsearch/reference/current/mapping.html

- **Elasticsearch Search API**: https://www.elastic.co/guide/en/
  elasticsearch/reference/current/search-search.html

 Elasticsearch should not be your primary data store. It does not provide guarantees, such as the **Atomicity, Consistency, Isolation, and Durability (ACID)** of a traditional SQL data store, nor the reliability guarantees of other NoSQL databases such as HBase or Cassandra. Even though Elasticsearch has built-in data redundancy and fault tolerance, it's best practice to archive your data in a separate data store in order to re-index data into Elasticsearch if needed.

# Similar technologies

This section explains a few of the many open source full-text search engines available, and discusses how they match up to Elasticsearch.

## Apache Lucene

Apache Lucene (https://lucene.apache.org/core/) is an open source full-text search Java library. As mentioned earlier, Lucene is Elasticsearch's underlying search technology. Lucene also provides Elasticsearch's analytics features such as text aggregations and geospatial search. Using Apache Lucene directly is a good choice if you perform full-text search in Java on a small scale, or are building your own full-text search engine.

The benefits of using Elasticsearch over Lucene are as follows:

- REST API instead of a Java API
- JSON document store
- Horizontal scalability, reliability, and fault tolerance

On the other hand, Lucene is much more lightweight and flexible to build custom applications that require full-text search integrated from the ground up.

Lucene.NET is a popular .NET port of the library written in C#

## Solr

Solr is another full-text search engine built on top of Apache Lucene. It has similar search, analytic, and scaling capabilities to Elasticsearch. For most applications that need a full-text search engine, choosing between Solr and Elasticsearch comes down to personal preference.

## Ferret

Ferret is a full-text search engine for Ruby. It's similar to Lucene, but it is not as feature-rich. It's generally better used for Ruby applications that don't require the power (or complexity) of a search engine, such as Elasticsearch or Solr.

# Monitoring Elasticsearch

Monitoring distributed systems is difficult because as the number of nodes, the number of users, and the amount of data increase, problems will begin to crop up.

Furthermore, it may not be immediately obvious if there is an error. Often, the cluster will keep running and try to recover from the error automatically. As shown in *Figures 1.2*, *1.3*, and *1.4* earlier, a node failed, but Elasticsearch brought itself back to a green state without any action on our part. Unless monitored, failures such as these can go unnoticed. This can have a detrimental impact on system performance and reliability. Fewer nodes means less processing power to respond to queries, and, as in the previous example, if another node fails, our cluster won't be able to return to a green state.

The aspects of an Elasticsearch cluster that we'll want to keep track of include the following:

- Cluster health and data availability
- Node failures
- Elasticsearch JVM memory usage
- Elasticsearch cache size
- System utilization (CPU, Memory, and Disk)
- Query response times
- Query rate

- Data index times
- Data index rate
- Number of indices and shards
- Index and shard size
- System configuration

In this book, we'll go over how to understand each of these variables in context and how understanding them can help diagnose, recover from, and prevent problems in our cluster. It's certainly not possible to preemptively stop all Elasticsearch errors. However, by proactively monitoring our cluster, we'll have a good idea of when things are awry and will be better positioned to take corrective action.

In the following chapters, we'll go over everything from web-based cluster monitoring tools to Unix command line tools and log file monitoring. Some of the specific tools this book covers are as follows:

- Elasticsearch-head
- Bigdesk
- Marvel
- Kopf
- Kibana
- Nagios
- Unix command-line tools

These tools will give us the information we need to effectively diagnose, solve, and prevent problems with Elasticsearch.

# Resourcefulness and problem solving

Monitoring tools do a great job of telling you what is going on in your cluster, and they can often point out if there is a problem. However, these tools won't give you a recipe for how to actually fix a problem. Resolving issues takes critical thinking, attention to detail, and persistence. Some of the problem-solving themes this book talks about are as follows:

- Always try to recreate the problem
- Be on the lookout for configuration and user errors
- Only make one configuration change at a time before testing

This book also provides some real-world case studies that help you turn the information provided by monitoring tools into insights to resolve Elasticsearch issues.

# Summary

This chapter gave you an overview of Elasticsearch and why it's important to proactively monitor a cluster. To summarize the points from the chapter:

- Elasticsearch is an open source scalable, fast, and fault-tolerant search engine
- Elasticsearch is built on top of Apache Lucene, the same library that powers Apache Solr
- Monitoring tools will help us get a better understanding of our cluster and will let us know when problems arise
- As helpful as monitoring tools are, it's up to us to actually diagnose and fix cluster issues

In the next chapter, we'll cover how to get a simple Elasticsearch cluster running and loaded with data, and how to install several monitoring tools.

# 2
# Installation and the Requirements for Elasticsearch

The **Java Runtime Environment** (**JRE**) is the only requirement to run Elasticsearch.

The official Elasticsearch documentation recommends that you use either Oracle Java 8 (update 20 or later), or Oracle Java 7 (update 55 or later). Once you choose your version of the JRE, we recommend that all your nodes use the same version to maintain compatibility. Using different versions of Java across your cluster or using Java versions earlier than the ones specified here, can lead to data corruption. Once you choose a version of Elasticsearch, all the nodes in your cluster should use the same version.

While it is possible to run Elasticsearch on both Windows and Linux, this book focuses on using it exclusively in a Linux environment. The Elasticsearch documentation is centered on Linux and most of the Elasticsearch community runs the software on Linux. However, there is no reason a production cluster of Elasticsearch cannot run on Windows.

This chapter will specifically cover installation instructions for Ubuntu, CentOS, and Red Hat Enterprise Linux (RHEL), but any Linux distribution will work. Readers should use 64-bit operating systems rather than 32-bit operating systems because the former allows more memory allocation for the JRE.

This chapter covers the following topics:

- Installing Elasticsearch
- Configuring Elasticsearch

- Installing monitoring tools (Elasticsearch-head, Bigdesk, and Marvel)
- Cluster requirements

# Installing Elasticsearch

At the time of writing this book, Elasticsearch 2.3.2 is the current stable release and Elasticsearch 5 is in alpha testing. For production clusters, we recommend using the 2.3.2 release and quickly updating to the 5 general availability (GA) release once it is available. Note that while Elasticsearch 5 is compatible with indices created in Elasticsearch 2.x, there have also been some API changes and feature deprecations after the 1.x release. Readers should account for these important changes before upgrading. More details on upgrading from 2.x to 5 can be found on the Elastic website at the following URLS:

- `https://www.elastic.co/blog/elasticsearch-5-0-0-alpha1-released`
- `https://www.elastic.co/blog/elasticsearch-5-0-0-alpha2-released`

Notable API changes include the following:

- Indices from Elasticsearch 1.x must first be upgraded to 2.x before finally moving to version 5
- The deprecated `filtered`, `or`, and `and` queries were removed in favor of the `bool`, `must`, and `should` queries
- The `string` mapping was deprecated in favor of the `text` and `keyword` fields
- The `index` mapping property is now set to `true` / `false` instead of `analyzed` / `not_analyzed` / `no`
- Significant changes to the Percolate API
- The `_id` values are limited to 512 bytes

While examples in this book use the 2.3.2 Elasticsearch release, all examples should be compatible with the upcoming 5.0 release.

The latest version of Elasticsearch is available at `https://www.elastic.co/downloads/elasticsearch` in `.zip`, `.tar.gz`, `.rpm`, and `.deb` formats. It doesn't matter how Elasticsearch is installed, but because it is simpler, we recommend using the `.deb` installer for Ubuntu users, the `.rpm` installer for CentOS or RHEL users, and the `.tar.gz` or `.zip` version for users of other Linux distributions, or for users who require a more customized setup. Elasticsearch also provides official `yum` and `apt-get` repositories.

Examples in this chapter assume that the user installed Elasticsearch with the `.rpm` or `.deb` installer, or through the official `yum` or `apt-get` repositories. This should also be similar for users who installed with the `.zip` and `.tar.gz` installers.

# DEB/RPM installation

First, download the most up-to-date package from `https://elastic.co`:

1. Run the following to install the DEB package on an Ubuntu or Debian-compatible system:

```
wget
  https://download.elastic.co/
  elasticsearch/elasticsearch/elasticsearch-2.3.2.deb

sudo dpkg -i elasticsearch-2.3.2.deb
```

2. Run the following to install the RPM package on a CentOS, RHEL, or another compatible system:

```
wget
  https://download.elastic.co/elasticsearch/elasticsearch/
  elasticsearch-2.3.2.noarch.rpm

sudo rpm -i elasticsearch-2.3.2.noarch.rpm
```

# The yum and apt-get repositories

The official `yum` and `apt-get` repositories are a great way to install Elasticsearch. However, make sure that you use the *official* repositories. Many third-party `yum` and `apt-get` Elasticsearch repositories are available, but they may not have the latest stable release.

# Ubuntu/Debian and apt-get

To install Elasticsearch using `apt-get` follow these steps:

1. To enable the repository via `apt-get`, first add the `gpg` key:

```
wget -qO - https://packages.elastic.co/GPG-KEY-elasticsearch |
  sudo apt-key add -
```

2. Then, add the repository via the following:

```
echo "deb http://packages.elastic.co/elasticsearch/2.3/debian
stable main" | sudo tee -a /etc/apt/sources.list.d/elasticsearch-
2.3.list
```

3. Finally, use your package manager to install the following:

```
sudo apt-get install elasticsearch
```

# CentOS/RHEL and yum

For yum, follow these steps:

1. Add the gpg key:

```
rpm --import https://packages.elastic.co/GPG-KEY-elasticsearch
```

2. Then, create a new yum repository at /etc/yum.repos.d/elasticsearch. repo with the following content:

```
[elasticsearch-2.3]
name=Elasticsearch 2.3.X repository
baseurl=http://packages.elastic.co/elasticsearch/2.3/centos
gpgcheck=1
gpgkey=http://packages.elastic.co/GPG-KEY-elasticsearch
enabled=1
```

3. Install the package with the following:

```
sudo yum install elasticsearch
```

# Verification

Start Elasticsearch with the following command:

```
sudo /etc/init.d/elasticsearch start
```

Then verify installation, test to see whether Elasticsearch is running and loaded via the following:

```
curl localhost:9200
```

You should get this response:

```
{
    "status" : 200,
    "name" : "Inertia",
    "cluster_name" : "Elasticsearch",
    "version" : {
        "number" : "2.3.2",
        "build_hash" : " b9e4a6acad4008027e4038f6abed7f7dba346f94",
```

```
        "build_timestamp" : "2016-04-21T16:03:47Z ",
        "build_snapshot" : false,
        "lucene_version" : "5.5.0"
    },
    "tagline" : "You Know, for Search"
}
```

To verify that we are able to write data to Elasticsearch, use the following:

```
curl -XPUT 'http://localhost:9200/twitter/user/lababidi'
  -d '{ "name" : "Mahmoud Lababidi" }'
```

This returns the following:

```
{"_index":"twitter","_type":"user","_id":"lababidi",
  "_version":1,"created":true}
```

We fetch the data, as follows:

```
curl -XGET 'http://localhost:9200/twitter/user/
  lababidi?pretty=true'
```

This returns the following output:

```
{
    "_index" : "twitter",
    "_type" : "user",
    "_id" : "lababidi",
    "_version" : 1,
    "found" : true,
    "_source":{ "name" : "Mahmoud Lababidi" }
}
```

As a sanity check, try a nonexisting record:

```
curl -XGET 'http://localhost:9200/twitter/user/
  kimchy?pretty=true'
```

This should return an expected `false` for `found`:

```
{
    "_index" : "twitter",
    "_type" : "user",
    "_id" : "kimchy",
    "found" : false
}
```

# Configuration files

It is worth noting the Elasticsearch installation location, specifically the configuration files and the log files. For example, on Ubuntu, run the following:

```
dpkg -L Elasticsearch
```

This will show that the installation placed the logs in `/var/log/elasticsearch` and the config files in `/etc/elasticsearch`. Any settings for Elasticsearch (not related to logging) are in `elasticsearch.yml` while `logging.yml` handles logging.

We will delve into these files and their respective settings further throughout the book.

# Configuring an Elasticsearch cluster

This section will cover some basic Elasticsearch configuration in addition to a few changes that will positively impact your cluster's performance.

Most Elasticsearch configuration changes will be applied to `elasticsearch.yml`. For our installation of Elasticsearch on Ubuntu, this file is located at `/etc/elasticsearch/elasticsearch.yml`. Elasticsearch internal configuration changes are applied to `elasticsearch.yml`. Environmental variables can be set in the application's startup script. For our installation of Elasticsearch 2.3.2 on Ubuntu, these files are in the following locations:

- Internal Configuration is located at

  `/etc/elasticsearch/elasticsearch.yml`

- Environmental Variable Configuration is located at

  `/etc/defaults/elasticsearch`

# Cluster name

A wonderful thing about Elasticsearch is the ease with which you can build a cluster. Elasticsearch nodes on the same local area network (LAN) will automatically form a cluster with each other if they have the configuration variable `cluster.name` set to the same value.

For example, if we store tweets from Twitter in our cluster, we may want to set `cluster.name` to `twitter_development`. Later on, we may want to create another cluster with the name `twitter_production` to hold all of our production data.

To modify this setting, edit the `Elasticsearch.yml` file and look for the `cluster.name` setting. Change this value to: `cluster.name: twitter_development`.

The default value for `cluster.name` is `elasticsearch`. It is fine to use this in solo development, but be careful using it when you are on a LAN with other developers. If you start a new Elasticsearch with the default `cluster.name` value and someone else on your network is also running Elasticsearch with the default configuration, you'll notice that data from their Elasticsearch instance will start replicating in your machine.

# Memory configuration

Elasticsearch recommends setting the heap size to half of the available RAM on the machine, but no more than 30.5 GB. We are using a machine with 16 GB of RAM, so we'll set the heap size to 8 GB. This configuration change is made to the `ES_HEAP_SIZE` environment variable in `/etc/defaykts/elasticsearch`:

```
ES_HEAP_SIZE=8g
```

# Open file limit

Linux limits the number of file descriptors a process can have open at one time. This limit exists because every time a process opens a file descriptor, it uses a little bit of memory. If there were no limit on the number of open files, a process could potentially open enough files to cause the entire system to run out of memory and crash.

By default, this limit is set to `1024`, which is too low for Elasticsearch. The official Elasticsearch documentation recommends upping this value to `32k` or `64k` for open files.

# The maximum file limit

The most up-to-date `.rpm` and `.deb` installers will automatically increase the maximum open file limit in Elasticsearch to `65535`. However, if you use an older version of the `.deb` or `.rpm`, or run Elasticsearch from the tarball, you'll have to increase the limit manually.

To check the maximum number of open files allocated to your current user, run the following:

```
$ ulimit -n
65535
```

The user has a maximum of `65535` files. However, this does *not* mean Elasticsearch is assigned this number of files. This may mean that Elasticsearch is running as a different user or that it was started with different environment settings.

To check the maximum number of open files allocated to Elasticsearch, run the following:

```
curl -XGET 'http://localhost:9200/
  _nodes?os=true&process=true&pretty=true'
```

The result should look something like this:

```
{
  "ok" : true,
  "cluster_name" : "Elasticsearch",
  "nodes" : {
    "-P1cQt91ThejPG_rj-reKw" : {
      "name" : "Korg",
      . . .
      "process" : {
        "refresh_interval" : 1000,
        "id" : 1407,
        "max_file_descriptors" : 1024
      }
    }
  }
}
```

We see that `max_file_descriptors` was set to `1024`, so we'll have to increase it. If your output says `65535`, skip to the next section.

Make sure that this is for the appropriate node; this `curl` command will display the `max_file` descriptors for all nodes in your cluster.

# Updating max file descriptors on Ubuntu Linux

Edit the `/etc/security/limits.conf` file and add the following lines to the end of the file:

```
*    soft    nofile 65536
*    hard    nofile 65536
```

> The * symbol means *all users*. You can also set this to just the user that runs the Elasticsearch process.

# Enabling pluggable authentication modules

If we connect to the Linux server over SSH, we'll have to ensure that PAM authentication is enabled. These instructions are the same if you use Ubuntu or CentOS/RHEL. To make this configuration change, edit the `sshd_config` file:

```
sudo vim /etc/ssh/sshd_config
```

Ensure that this line is present:

```
UsePAM yes
```

Then, restart your SSH server:

```
sudo service ssh restart
```

# Verifying the open file limit

Log out and log back in again to make these changes take effect, then restart the Elasticsearch server:

```
exit
ssh <your_username>@<your_server>
sudo service elasticsearch restart
```

Finally, be sure to verify that these changes took effect. It is not enough to verify that `ulimit -n` returns `65536`. It is also important to ensure that the Elasticsearch user was started up properly with the increased maximum open file limit:

```
curl -XGET 'http://localhost:9200/
  _nodes?os=true&process=true&pretty=true'
```

This should result in the following:

```
{
  "ok" : true,
  "cluster_name" : "Elasticsearch",
  "nodes" : {
    "-P1cQt9lThejPG_rj-reKw" : {
      "name" : "Korg",
      ...
      "process" : {
        "refresh_interval" : 1000,
        "id" : 1407,
```

```
      "max_file_descriptors" : 65536
    }
  }
}
```

This time we see that max_file_descriptors is set to 65536.

# Disabling swapping

It is important to disable memory swapping on your operating system or Elasticsearch process.

To disable swapping until your system is rebooted, run the following:

```
sudo swapoff -a
```

To disable swapping even after your system is rebooted, edit the /etc/fstab file, and comment out any lines with the word swap in them. For us, this looked like the following:

```
# /dev/xvdb    none         swap
  sw                        0 0
```

To disable swap for just Elasticsearch, you'll first have to set your Elasticsearch heap size using ES_HEAP_SIZE and set the process maximum amount of locked memory to ulimited as the root user. If you use the .rpm or .deb installer, both of these settings can be changed in the /etc/init.d/elasticsearch startup script. Specifically, uncomment and update these lines, as follows:

(My machine has 512 MB of memory, so I'm setting ES_HEAP_SIZE to 256m.)

```
# Set ES_HEAP_SIZE to 50% of available RAM, but no more than 31g
ES_HEAP_SIZE=256m
```

A little further down:

```
# Maximum amount of locked memory
MAX_LOCKED_MEMORY=unlimited
```

Next, edit your elasticsearch.yml file, and add the line:

```
bootstrap.mlockall: true
```

Then, reboot your Elasticsearch node:

```
sudo service elasticsearch restart
```

Finally, verify that this setting worked by running the following:

```
curl http://localhost:9200/_nodes/process?pretty
```

You should see the following:

```
"mlockall" : true
```

This is the response.

# Understanding your cluster

Elasticsearch has many different moving parts, and it can get a little complicated to ensure that everything runs properly. Fortunately, there are some great open source monitoring tools that are available to help you keep tabs on your cluster. This section will cover how to install some of the most popular and useful monitoring tools on your cluster, and the following two chapters will go into these tools in more detail.

## Installing Elasticsearch-head

Elasticsearch-head is a simple, free, open source tool that provides a high-level examination of your cluster. It is one of the most useful tools used when administering and monitoring the health of a cluster. Elasticsearch-head only needs to be installed on one node in your cluster. However, we recommend installing it on all nodes for redundancy. It's installed as an Elasticsearch plugin.

If you have an Internet connection, you can install Elasticsearch-head with the Elasticsearch `plugin` utility, as follows:

```
sudo /usr/share/elasticsearch/bin/plugin
  install mobz/elasticsearch-head
```

The location of the `plugin` script may vary.

The next command assumes that you installed Elasticsearch using the `.rpm` or `.deb` file, but if you are unsure where the plugin script is in your installation, go ahead and try running the following commands:

```
sudo updatedb
```
```
locate elasticsearch | grep plugin$
```

For me, this returns the following:

```
/usr/share/elasticsearch/bin/plugin
```

If you don't have an Internet connection on your Elasticsearch instance, you can download the Elasticsearch-head plugin, transfer it to your server, and install it using the following methods.

From a machine with an Internet connection, we use the following:

```
wget https://github.com/mobz/elasticsearch-head/archive/
  master.zip -O Elasticsearch-head.zip
scp Elasticsearch-head.zip your_server:~/
```

From the Elasticsearch server, we use the following:

```
sudo /usr/share/elasticsearch/bin/plugin
  install file:///path/to/Elasticsearch-head.zip
```

If you run an old version of Elasticsearch, you may have to restart your node before you can open Elasticsearch-head:

```
sudo service elasticsearch restart
```

Try out the plugin by visiting `http://elasticsearch-server:9200/_plugin/head/` (for a test environment, `elasticsearch-server` is probably `localhost`). You should see something like the following:

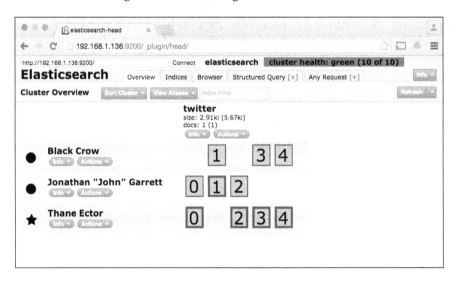

# Installing Bigdesk

Bigdesk is a free, open source Elasticsearch plugin that allows you to see your cluster's CPU, memory, and disk usage. It's a great tool to dig into performance issues with a cluster and, like Elasticsearch-head, it only needs to be installed on one node in your cluster. We still recommend installing it on all nodes for redundancy.

Here's how to install Bigdesk.

Online installation is as follows:

```
sudo /usr/share/elasticsearch/bin/plugin
  install AIsaac08/bigdesk
```

Offline installation is has more than one method.

From a machine with an Internet connection, use the following:

```
wget https://github.com/AIsaac08/bigdesk/zipball/master -O bigdesk.zip
scp bigdesk.zip your_server:~/
```

From the Elasticsearch server, use the following:

```
sudo /usr/share/elasticsearch/bin/plugin
  install file:///path/to/bigdesk.zip
```

As with Elasticsearch-head, if you run an old version of Elasticsearch, you may have to restart your node before you can open Bigdesk:

```
sudo service elasticsearch restart
```

Try out the plugin by visiting `http://elasticsearch-server:9200/_plugin/ bigdesk/` (for a test environment, elasticsearch-server is probably localhost). You should see something like the following:

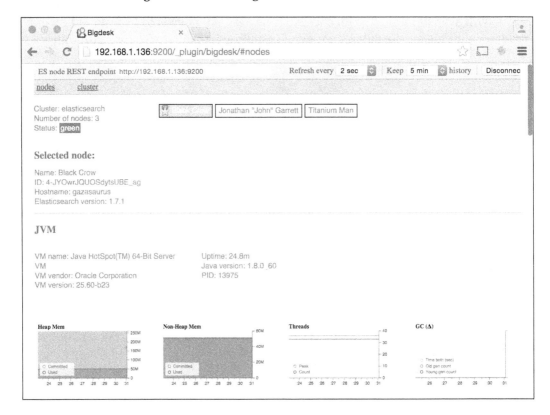

# Marvel

Marvel is a powerful monitoring tool created by the makers of Elasticsearch. It's free for use in development, but there's a subscription fee to use it in production. Marvel consists of the following two components:

1. Marvel Agent (requires Marvel License).
2. Marvel Dashboard (requires Kibana).

To install the Marvel Agent:

- Online installation is as follows:

```
sudo /usr/share/elasticsearch/bin/plugin install license
sudo /usr/share/elasticsearch/bin/
  plugin install marvel-agent
```

- Offline installation is as follows:

```
wget https://download.elastic.co/elasticsearch/release/org/
  elasticsearch/plugin/license/2.3.3/license-2.3.3.zip
```

```
wget https://download.elastic.co/elasticsearch/release/org/
  elasticsearch/plugin/marvel-agent/2.3.3/
  marvel-agent-2.3.3.zip
```

```
sudo bin/plugin install file:
  ///absolute/path/to /license-2.3.3.zip
```

```
sudo bin/plugin install file:
  ///absolute/path/to/marvel-agent-2.3.3.zip
```

Restart Elasticsearch after installing the Marvel Agent:

```
sudo service elasticsearch restart
```

To install the Marvel Dashboard, use the following steps:

1. First, install Kibana:

```
wget https://download.elastic.co/
  kibana/kibana/kibana-4.5.1-linux-x64.tar.gz
```

```
tar xzvf kibana-4.5.1-linux-x64.tar.gz
```

2. Next, install the Marvel Dashboard as a Kibana plugin:

```
cd kibana-4.5.1
```

```
wget https://download.elasticsearch.org/
  elasticsearch/marvel/marvel-2.3.3.tar.gz
```

```
bin/kibana plugin
  --install marvel --url file:///tmp/marvel-2.3.3.tar.gz
```

3. Start Kibana:

```
./bin/kibana
```

4. Open the Marvel Dashboard by visiting `http://server-name:5601/` (for a test environment, `server-name` is probably `localhost`). You should see something like the following:

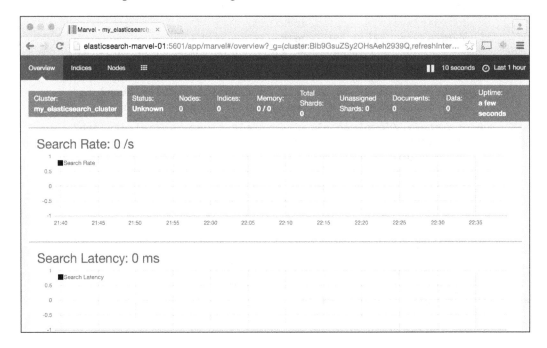

# Cluster requirements

The requirements for your cluster—the number of nodes and the hardware specifications of each node—depend on several factors, including the following:

- Total volume of data
- Data ingest rate
- Average record size
- Data mapping
- Types of queries being run
- System performance requirements

There's no one size fits all formula to determine cluster requirements for a given Elasticsearch use case. The best approach is to meticulously test performance while changing variables, such as shard size, the number of nodes in the cluster, and hardware configurations until an optimal solution is found. This section focuses on high-level guidelines to consider when configuring your cluster.

It's a good idea to run at least three nodes in a production environment and to set data replication to *1*, which asks Elasticsearch to maintain one copy of each shard in the cluster. This configuration will ensure that if a node goes down, your cluster won't lose any data.

Elasticsearch tends to be more memory intensive than CPU intensive. Any modern 64-bit processor is likely adequate to run Elasticsearch. In general, this favors more processor cores over faster clock speeds.

Each node in the cluster should have minimum 512 MB of RAM, and half of this should be allocated to Elasticsearch. The Elasticsearch documentation recommends allocating no more than 30.5 GB of memory to an Elasticsearch node because the JVM compresses internally stored memory addresses when heap sizes are less than 30.5 GB but is no longer able to do so when the allocated heap is larger than 30.5 GB. A good rule of thumb is to have no more than 64 GB of total memory per node. Moreover, when determining your total memory requirement for a cluster, you will likely need much less total system memory than your total index size, but the specific amount will vary depending on your use case.

When considering storage for an Elasticsearch cluster, prefer internal drives to **network attached storage (NAS)** solutions. Using solid-state drives instead of traditional hard drives will greatly improve overall system performance.

# Summary

This chapter covered Elasticsearch installation, configuration, monitoring tools, and cluster requirements. Tools such as Elasticsearch-head, Bigdesk, and Marvel all lay the groundwork to monitor your cluster and analyze its performance. However, you still have to know what aspects to look for and how to find them. In the next chapter, we will examine Elasticsearch-head and Bigdesk further, and discuss important things to look for in these tools when monitoring an Elasticsearch cluster.

# 3
# Elasticsearch-head and Bigdesk

This chapter talks about the Elasticsearch monitoring plugins Elasticsearch-head and Bigdesk, along with the Elasticsearch cat API. These utilities are used to assess the status of your cluster and to diagnose issues:

- **Elasticsearch-head**: This is used to get an idea of your overall cluster health, individual node status, and an understanding of your indices
- **Bigdesk**: This is used to look into the memory, disk, and CPU usage of individual nodes in your cluster
- **Elasticsearch cat API**: This lets you access many of Elasticsearch's internal metrics without installing any plugins

Specifically, this chapter explores the following:

- Configuring an Elasticsearch cluster
- Loading sample data into Elasticsearch
- Using Elasticsearch-head
- Using Bigdesk
- The Elasticsearch cat API

## Cluster setup

This section covers configuring a three-node Elasticsearch cluster and loading it with Twitter data.

# Cluster configuration

Setting up an Elasticsearch cluster is simple. All nodes in the cluster should be on the same local network and have the same version of Java and Elasticsearch installed. For our cluster, we'll use three Ubuntu Linux 14.04 virtual hosts: `elasticsearch-node-01`, `elasticsearch-node-02`, and `elasticsearch-node-03`.

After installing Elasticsearch on all hosts, update the `elasticsearch.yml` configuration file on each, as follows:

- The configuration for `elasticsearch-node-01` is as follows:

```
cluster.name: my_elasticsearch_cluster
node.name: "elasticsearch-node-01"
discovery.zen.ping.multicast.enabled: false
discovery.zen.ping.unicast.hosts: ["elasticsearch-node-02",
"elasticsearch-node-03"]
index.routing.allocation.disable_allocation: false
cluster.routing.allocation.enable : all
```

- The configuration for `elasticsearch-node-02` is as follows:

```
cluster.name: my_elasticsearch_cluster
node.name: "elasticsearch-node-02"
discovery.zen.ping.multicast.enabled: false
discovery.zen.ping.unicast.hosts: ["elasticsearch-node-01",
"elasticsearch-node-03"]
index.routing.allocation.disable_allocation: false
cluster.routing.allocation.enable : all
```

- The configuration for `elasticsearch-node-03` is as follows:

```
cluster.name: my_elasticsearch_cluster
node.name: "elasticsearch-node-03"
discovery.zen.ping.multicast.enabled: false
discovery.zen.ping.unicast.hosts: ["elasticsearch-node-01",
"elasticsearch-node-02"]
index.routing.allocation.disable_allocation: false
cluster.routing.allocation.enable : all
```

Next, install Elasticsearch-head on all nodes in this cluster using the instructions found in the previous chapter.

Now, restart all nodes and verify that the cluster is properly formed by visiting Elasticsearch-head at `http://elasticsearch-node-01:9200/_plugin/head/`.

You should see something like this, with all of your cluster's nodes listed in the leftmost column:

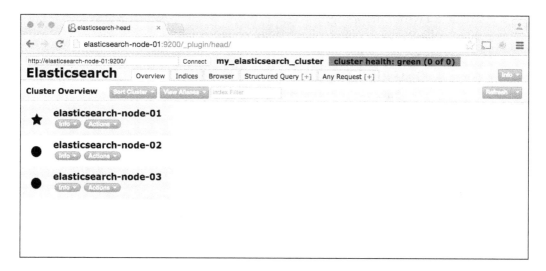

# Sample data

Now that we have a cluster up and running, let's populate it with Twitter data. We use Twitter data as an example because it is easy to acquire in large quantities and because it is a continuously-flowing stream of information, which is similar to a lot of real-world datasets.

Use the Elasticsearch `stream2es` utility to get the Twitter data. This utility is available at `https://github.com/elastic/stream2es`:

1. Create a new Twitter account or log into your Twitter account if you already have one.

2. Associate your mobile phone number with the account at `https://support.twitter.com/articles/110250`.

3. Create a new Twitter application at `https://apps.twitter.com/app/new`.

> 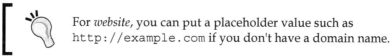 For *website*, you can put a placeholder value such as `http://example.com` if you don't have a domain name.

4. Make a note of your **Consumer Key (API Key)** and **Consumer Secret (API Secret)** in the **Keys and Access Tokens** tab:

   ```
   ./stream2es twitter --authorize --key CONSUMER_KEY --secret
   CONSUMER_SECRET
   ```

5.  Authorize the app.

6.  Enter the verification code.

7.  Create a Twitter mapping:

```
curl -XPUT 'http://localhost:9200/twitter/' -d '{
    "settings" : {
        "index" : {
            "number_of_shards" : 3,
            "number_of_replicas" : 1
        }
    }
}'
```

8.  Collect tweets:

```
./stream2es twitter --target http://localhost:9200/twitter/status
--settings '{
    "settings" : {
        "index" : {
            "number_of_shards" : 3,
            "number_of_replicas" : 2
        }
    }
}'
```

9.  Take a look at the tweets coming in:

```
curl -XGET "http://localhost:9200/twitter/_search?size=0&pretty"
```

After letting `stream2es` run for a while, we get the following:

```
{
  "took" : 63,
  "timed_out" : false,
  "_shards" : {
    "total" : 3,
    "successful" : 3,
    "failed" : 0
  },
  "hits" : {
    "total" : 150765,
    "max_score" : 0.0,
    "hits" : [ ]
```

```
    }
  }
```

Now that we have populated our cluster with some sample data, we can discuss how to use Elasticsearch-head, Bigdesk, and the Elasticsearch cat API.

# Elasticsearch-head

In *Chapter 2*, *Installation and the Requirements for Elasticsearch*, we introduced and installed Elasticsearch-head, and now we will begin examining its features.

# The Overview tab

The first tab in Elasticsearch-head is the **Overview** tab. This tab answers questions such as the following:

- How many nodes are in the cluster?
- Is the cluster in a healthy state?
- Is all of the cluster's data available?
- How many indices are in the cluster, and how big are they?
- How much data is in the cluster?

Users can also use this tab to perform some basic administrative actions (creating indices, deleting indices, and so on).

After loading in sample Twitter data from the previous section, our **Overview** tab looks like the following:

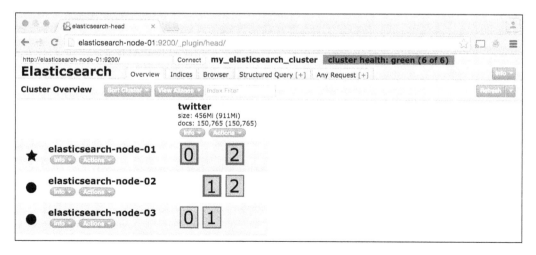

We can see that three nodes are up and running:

- `elasticsearch-node-01`
- `elasticsearch-node-02`
- `elasticsearch-node-03`

We also have one active index that contains our newly loaded Twitter data. From this page, we can tell the following:

- The Twitter index takes up 456 MB
- The Twitter index contains 150,765 documents

# Cluster states

An Elasticsearch cluster can be in any of these three states:

- **Green**: All data is available and all shard replicas are assigned.

 The previous screenshot tells that we are currently in a `green` state.

- **Yellow**: All data is available, but not all replicas are assigned:
    - This usually happens in a one-node cluster when you have a replica size of > 0, or in a multi node cluster right after a node goes down.
    - If a node in your cluster goes down, a `yellow` state will resolve itself after all replica shards are re-assigned.
    - Elasticsearch will automatically try to reassign shards after a default 1-minute wait time to see if the problematic node reappears.

- **Red**: Not all data is available, and not all shards are assigned.
    - This state deserves immediate attention. This is usually caused by multiple node failures at once due to a simultaneous restart, power failure, or network failure in your cluster.
    - The best way to resolve this state is to bring all of the down nodes in your cluster back up.
    - Note that even in a `red` state, Elasticsearch will still return query results. However, query counts will be inaccurate.

For the purposes of demonstration, we'll shut down `elasticsearch-node-02` and `elasticsearch-node-03` to get a sense of what the cluster looks like in different states:

- Shut down `elasticsearch-node-02`:

  ```
  ssh elasticsearchn-node-02
  sudo /etc/init.d/elasticsearch stop
  ```

- Refresh Elasticsearch-head. We should see something like this:

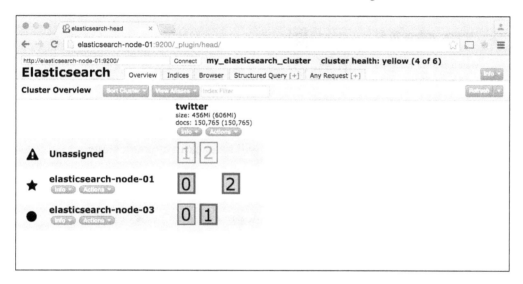

Note that `elasticsearch-node-02` is no longer present, and that the cluster is in a `yellow` state.

Remember that a `yellow` state means that all data is still available. More node failures may result in a `red` state or data being unavailable.

After waiting a few minutes, Elasticsearch will start to reassign these shards to the remaining hosts:

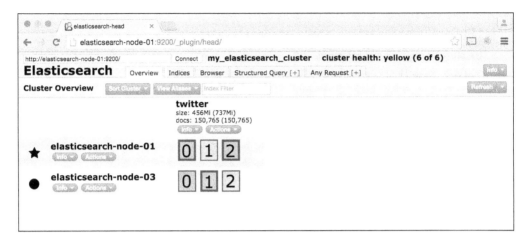

After reassignment is complete; the cluster will be back in a green state:

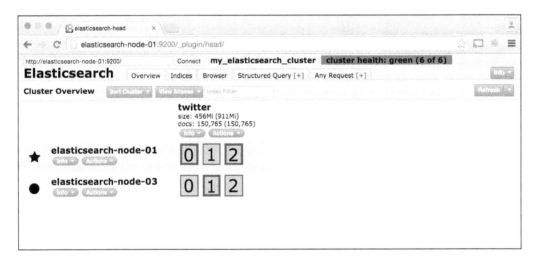

Let's experiment and turn the cluster into a red state:

1. Turn elasticsearch-node-02 back on and wait until elasticsearch-node-02 has a few shards assigned to it.

2. Once this happens, shut down both elasticsearch-node-02 and elasticsearch-node-03 without giving the cluster time to reassign shards.

3. You can do this on Elasticsearch-head by selecting **Shutdown** from **Actions** next to each respective node or on the command line:

```
ssh elasticsearchn-node-02
sudo /etc/init.d/elasticsearch stop
ssh elasticsearchn-node-03
sudo /etc/init.d/elasticsearch stop
```

4. After shutting down these nodes and refreshing Elasticsearch-head, we'll see something like this:

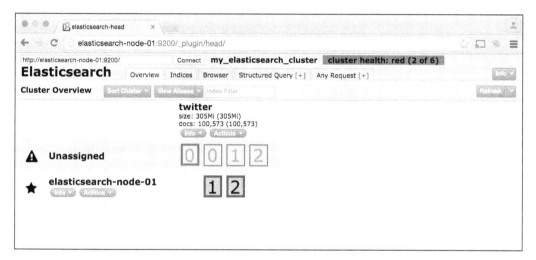

5. Note that only shards 1 and 2 in the Twitter index are assigned, and shard 0 is unassigned. As a result, the index size and document counts have decreased from 456 MB to 305 MB and 150,765 to 100,573, respectively.

6. Once we restart `elasticsearch-node-02` and `elasticsearch-node-03`, the cluster will recover and return to a `green` state.

# Node and index actions

Next to the name of each node and index, you'll see dropdowns labeled **Info** and **Actions**. Each of the links in these dropdowns corresponds to various Elasticsearch API calls:

- The **Info** links all return **JSON** documents with details about the status of your index or node

- The **Actions** links provide convenience methods to manipulate your cluster

The following table goes into more detail about each of these links:

| Target (Index or Node) | Type (action or info) | Name (for example, "Node Stats") | Elasticsearch API methods | Description |
|---|---|---|---|---|
| Node | Info | Cluster Node Info | `GET /_nodes` | This provides the node's Elasticsearch configuration, installed plugins, and the server's available memory, CPU, and disk space. |
| Node | Info | Node Stats | `GET /_nodes/ stats?all=true` | This provides counts and statistics of the number of Elasticsearch documents stored on the node. Also provides JVM, network, and filesystem metrics. |
| Node | Action | Shutdown | `POST /_cluster/ nodes/<NODE_ID>/_ shutdown` | This shuts down the Elasticsearch process on the specified node. |
| Index | Info | Index Status | `GET /_status` | This provides information about the specified index, such as the state, number of documents, size, and various other metrics. |
| Index | Info | Index Metadata | `GET /_cluster/ state` | This provides the index's mapping, aliases, and settings. |
| Index | Actions | New Alias... | `POST /_aliases` | This creates a new index alias. |
| Index | Actions | Refresh | `POST /<INDEX_ NAME>/_refresh` | This refreshes the index. |
| Index | Actions | Flush | `POST /<INDEX_ NAME>/_flush` | This flushes the index. |
| Index | Actions | Optimize... | `POST /<INDEX_ NAME>/_optimize` | This optimizes the index. |
| Index | Actions | Gateway Snapshot | `POST /<INDEX_ NAME>/_gateway/ snapshot` | This takes a snapshot of the index. |

| Target (Index or Node) | Type (action or info) | Name (for example, "Node Stats") | Elasticsearch API methods | Description |
|---|---|---|---|---|
| Index | Actions | Test Analyzer | `GET /<INDEX_ NAME>/_ analyze?text=TEXT` | This analyzes the passed in text using the index's default text analyzer. |
| Index | Actions | Close | `POST /<INDEX_ NAME>/_analyze` | This closes an open index. |
| Index | Actions | Open | `POST /<INDEX_ NAME>/_open` | This opens a closed index. |
| Index | Actions | Delete | `POST /<INDEX_ NAME>/_delete` | This deletes an index. |

The **Info** actions just listed (**Cluster Node Info**, **Node Stats**, **Index Status**, and **Index Metadata**) provide a plethora of information about the state of your cluster and data holdings. However, looking at the JSON responses for these items can be a little overwhelming.

Bigdesk is the next tool that we'll look at in this chapter. Both Bigdesk and Marvel, a tool that we'll examine in the next chapter, take many of these metrics and display them in easy-to-read charts and graphs.

# The Indices tab

The **Indices** tab provides a list of the indices in your cluster, their disk size usage, and the number of documents in each. It is also a way to create a new index.

This tab doesn't offer any additional information about an index beyond what is provided in the **Overview** tab.

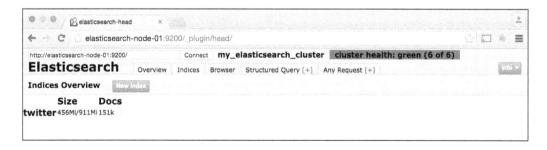

# The Browser tab

This tab lets you browse, view, and run basic filter queries against the documents in your indices. The following screenshot is an example of what a document view will look like in the **Browser** tab:

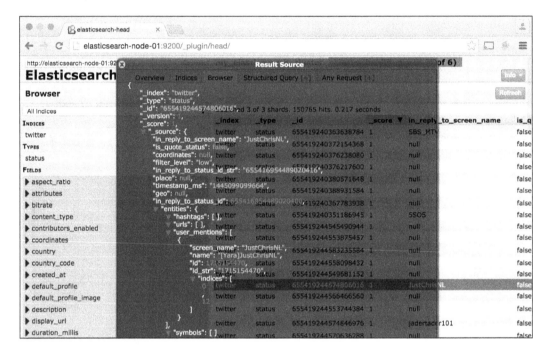

# The Structured Query tab

The **Structured Query** tab is an advanced query builder to explore the documents in your index. This tab is useful when you want to build a complex query without writing out the full JSON request body.

The following screenshot shows a sample query and results created using this interface:

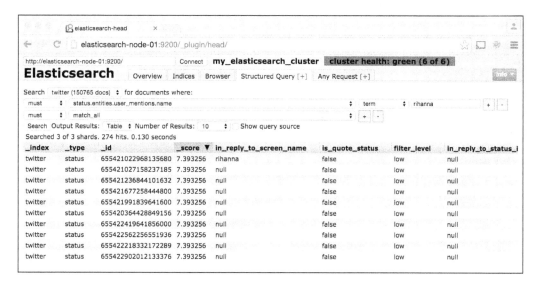

# The Any Request tab

The **Any Request** tab allows you to run arbitrary **API** calls against your cluster and view the results in **JSON**. The following screenshot shows a sample aggregation query:

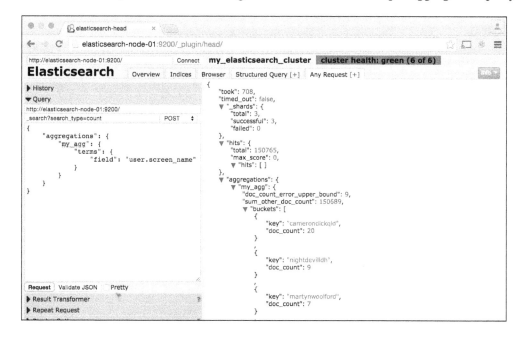

# The official website

For more information about Elasticsearch-head, visit the plugin's website at
`https://mobz.github.io/elasticsearch-head/`.

# Bigdesk

Bigdesk is a tool to look into various JVM and operating-system level metrics about
your cluster. If your cluster runs slowly or experiences unusual errors, Bigdesk is a
good place to check for anything out of the ordinary.

After following the installation instructions from the previous chapter, access
Bigdesk by visiting `http://elasticsearch-node-01:9200/plugin/bigdesk/`.
The initial landing page looks like this:

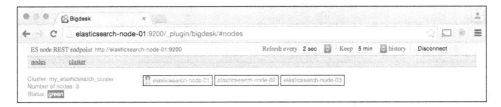

Like Elasticsearch-head, this page shows the nodes in your cluster and the cluster
health. Click on any of the nodes listed in the top row to display its individual
metrics:

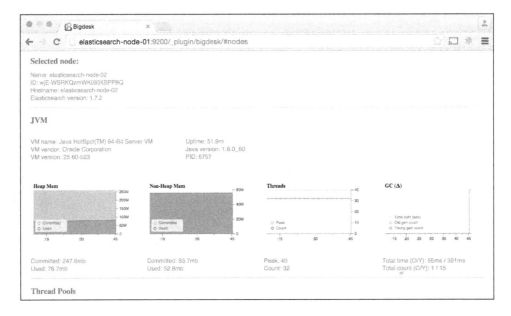

In this screenshot, we selected `elasticsearch-node-02` and are looking at **JVM** metrics. A notable chart in this section is the **Heap Mem** figure. If you are using close to the maximum amount of committed heap memory, you will want to increase your heap memory by setting `ES_HEAP_SIZE` to at the most half of your total available memory.

Further down, we see operating system metrics, namely:

- CPU usage
- Memory usage
- Swap space usage
- Load average

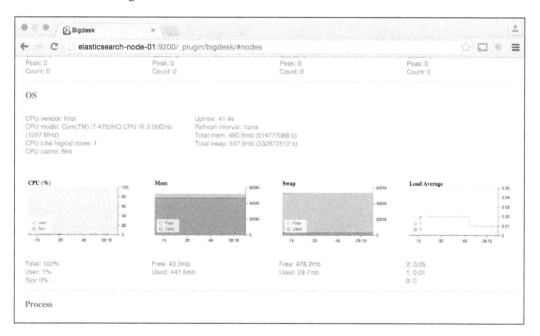

Below operating system metrics, we come to process level metrics, including the following:

- Open file descriptors
- Process memory usage
- CPU usage

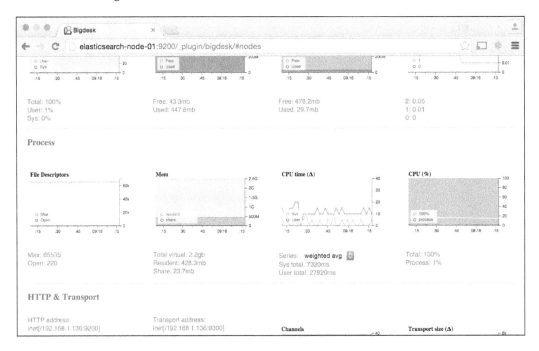

Refer to the operating system and process metrics charts if you are experiencing slow queries or slow data index operations to get a sense of the performance bottleneck.

Continuing down the page, we'll see some more notable charts, including:

- Cache size
- Indexing operations
- Filesystem activity

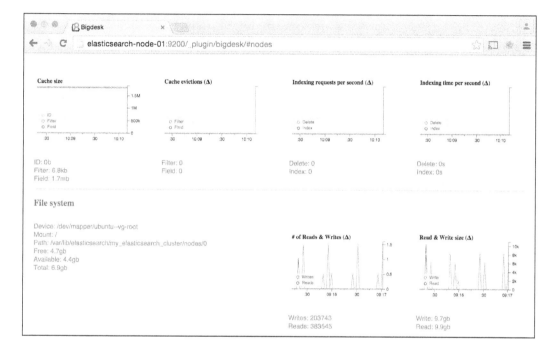

The **Cache size** chart is an important figure in this screenshot. The **ID**, **Filter**, and **Field** caches can fill up based on the type of queries you run. If they get too large, look at your queries for possible modifications to keep cache sizes down.

The Bigdesk charts are also useful for finding configuration errors. For example, if we meant to configure our node to use 32GB of memory and a maximum of 65535 open file descriptors, but the **JVM Heap Mem** chart shows only show 247MB of committed memory and the **Process File Descriptors** chart shows a limit of 1024 files, we'll know we didn't configure the node correctly.

 For more information about Bigdesk, visit the plugin's website at http://bigdesk.org/.

# The Elasticsearch cat API

Think of the **Elasticsearch cat API** as a simpler version of the **Elasticsearch Cluster** and **Indices APIs** mentioned earlier. The cat API returns results in an easy-to-read, tab-separated format, unlike the JSON returned by the Cluster and Indices APIs.

A complete list of API methods is available at `https://www.elastic.co/blog/introducing-cat-api`, but there are some highlights, which we cover in the following sections.

# Background

Elasticsearch-head and Bigdesk are, for the most part, powered by the Elasticsearch APIs:

- **Cluster API**: `https://www.elastic.co/guide/en/elasticsearch/reference/1.7/cluster.html`.

- **Indices API**: `https://www.elastic.co/guide/en/elasticsearch/reference/1.7/indices.html`.

These two APIs provide a plethora of information about the inner workings of Elasticsearch. However, they also return large *JSON* documents that are complicated to interpret quickly. For example, here's a snippet from calling the Indices Stats API:

```
curl -XGET "http://elasticsearch-node-01:9200/_stats?pretty"
{
  ...
  "_all" : {
    "primaries" : {
      "store" : {
        "size_in_bytes" : 477638305,
        "throttle_time_in_millis" : 0
      },
    ...
```

It's probably not immediately clear that the `size_in_bytes` value of `477638305` translates to 455 MB.

# Count

This endpoint provides a document count for the entire cluster:

```
curl -XGET http://elasticsearch-node-01:9200/_cat/count?v
```

This gives the output:

```
epoch         timestamp count
1445910583 21:49:43   150765
```

 Passing the v option to the cat API shows a header row.

The output columns represent the following:

- `epoch`: This represents a Unix timestamp
- `timestamp`: This represents the time of day
- `count`: This represents the number of documents in the cluster

# Health

This endpoint shows the health color code for the cluster:

```
curl -XGET http://elasticsearch-node-01:9200/_cat/health?v
```

This gives the output:

```
epoch         timestamp
  cluster                        status
  node.total node.data shards
  pri relo init unassign pending_tasks
1445910646 21:50:46
  my_elasticsearch_cluster green
  3         3       6
  3   0   0       0             0
```

These columns represent the following:

- `epoch`: This represents a Unix timestamp
- `timestamp`: This represents the time of day
- `cluster`: This represents a cluster name
- `status`: This represents a cluster status (green, yellow, or red)

- `node.total`: This represents the number of nodes in the cluster
- `node.data`: This represents the number of data nodes in the cluster
- `shards`: This represents the number of total shards in the cluster
- `pri`: This represents the number of primary shards (as opposed to replica shards)
- `relo`: This represents the number of shards currently relocating
- `init`: This represents the number of shards currently initializing
- `unassign`: This represents the number of unassigned shards
- `pending_tasks`: This represents the number of cluster tasks in the backlog

# Indices

This endpoint provides a list of all indices, their document count, and size in your cluster:

```
curl -XGET http://elasticsearch-node-01:9200/_cat/indices?v
```

This gives the output:

```
health status index pri rep docs.count docs.deleted
   store.size pri.store.size
green  open    twitter  3  1      150765              0
   911mb          455.5mb
```

This output has one line for each index in the cluster. The output columns represent the following:

- `health`: This is index health (`green`, `yellow`, or `red`)
- `status`: This indicates whether the index is open or closed
- `index`: This is the index name
- `pri`: This is the number of primary shards
- `rep`: This is the replication level (`1` means all shards are replicated once)
- `docs.count`: This is the number of documents in this index
- `docs.deleted`: This is the number of deleted documents
- `store.size`: This is the total index size
- `pri.store.size`: This is the size of index without replicas

# Shards

This endpoint provides a list of index shards and how they are distributed:

```
curl -XGET http://elasticsearch-node-01:9200/_cat/shards?v
```

This gives the output:

```
index     shard prirep state      docs    store ip
  node
twitter 0     r        STARTED 50192 150.2mb 127.0.1.1
  elasticsearch-node-03
twitter 0     p        STARTED 50192 150.2mb 192.168.56.1
  elasticsearch-node-01
twitter 1     p        STARTED 50305   152mb 127.0.1.1
  elasticsearch-node-03
twitter 1     r        STARTED 50305   152mb 127.0.1.1
  elasticsearch-node-02
twitter 2     p        STARTED 50268 153.2mb 127.0.1.1
  elasticsearch-node-02
twitter 2     r        STARTED 50268 153.2mb 192.168.56.1
  elasticsearch-node-01
```

Each row in this output is for a single shard in the cluster. The columns represent the following:

- index: This is the index name
- shard: This is the shard number
- prirep: This is p if a primary shard, r if a replica
- state: This is the availability of the shard
- docs: This is the number of documents in this shard
- store: This is the size of the shard on disk
- ip: This is the IP address where the shard is located
- node: This is the node name where the shard is located

# Summary

This chapter discussed how to configure and load data into a three-node Elasticsearch cluster. Additionally, it covered how to monitor a cluster using Elasticsearch-head, Bigdesk, and the cat API.

The next chapter will discuss Marvel—the official Elasticsearch monitoring tool.

# 4
# Marvel Dashboard

The previous two chapters covered Elasticsearch-head and Bigdesk, two open source monitoring tools. This chapter covers Marvel, a non-free tool for monitoring Elasticsearch.

Unlike Elasticsearch-head and Bigdesk, Marvel continuously captures and saves performance metrics to an index. This lets users refer to historical data for analysis, as opposed to just real-time data analysis. In this chapter, we will look a bit closer at the following topics:

- Setting up Marvel
- Upgrading Marvel
- Configuring Marvel
- Marvel index configuration
- Marvel dashboard
- Monitoring node failures

## Setting up Marvel

See *Chapter 2, Installation and the Requirements for Elasticsearch*, for instructions on how to install the Marvel Agent and the Marvel Kibana dashboard.

Marvel stores its metrics data inside Elasticsearch. It is possible to store these metrics alongside production data in the same Elasticsearch cluster; however, this is inadvisable because:

- Marvel's data indices can grow quite large and, in a production setting, you won't want these indices affecting the performance of your primary cluster.
- If the primary cluster is experiencing issues, having Marvel on a separate cluster will allow you to more easily diagnose those issues.

- If Marvel is running on a normal data node, it can inadvertently be configured to collect data on its own metrics indices. For example, if you log in to the Marvel dashboard and start querying the Marvel indices, these queries will then be logged back to the Marvel indices. This is probably not the intended behavior.

For these reasons, this chapter covers how to set up a separate Elasticsearch cluster for storing Marvel metrics data. Our primary Elasticsearch cluster from the last chapter contains three data nodes: `elasticsearch-node-01`, `elasticsearch-node-02`, and `elasticsearch-node-03`. We'll add a new cluster with a single Elasticsearch node to store Marvel's data.

Follow these steps to create a new Elasticsearch cluster for Marvel data:

1. On a new host called `elasticsearch-marvel-01`, install Elasticsearch 2.3.2 using the instructions from *Chapter 2, Installation and the Requirements for Elasticsearch*.

2. Configure Elasticsearch by editing the `elasticsearch.yml` configuration file to look like this:

   ```
   index.routing.allocation.disable_allocation: false

   cluster.routing.allocation.enable : all

   marvel.agent.enabled: false

   cluster.name: my_monitoring_cluster

   node.name: elasticsearch-marvel-01

   bootstrap.mlockall: true

   discovery.zen.ping.multicast.enabled: false
   ```

3. Install Elasticsearch-head on `elasticsearch-marvel-01`:

   ```
   sudo /usr/share/elasticsearch/bin/plugin
       install mobz/elasticsearch-head
   ```

4. Install the Marvel Agent on the three primary Elasticsearch nodes (`elasticsearch-node-01`, `elasticsearch-node-02`, and `elasticsearch-node-03`). Log in to each host and run the following command to install Marvel:

   ```
   sudo /usr/share/elasticsearch/bin/plugin install license
   sudo /usr/share/elasticsearch/bin/plugin install marvel-agent
   ```

As mentioned in *Chapter 2, Installation and the Requirements for Elasticsearch*, make sure to restart each node after installing Marvel, in order to get the Marvel agent started.

5. Add the following lines of configuration to the `elasticsearch.yml` in each of the original three `elasticsearch-node-0*` nodes:

```
marvel.agent.exporters:

  my_monitoring_cluster:

    type: http

    host: ["http://elasticsearch-marvel-01:9200"]
```

6. For a larger Marvel cluster with three nodes, for example, the configuration line might look like this:

```
marvel.agent.exporters:

  my_monitoring_cluster:

    type: http

    host: ["elasticsearch-marvel-01:9200",
      "elasticsearch-marvel-02:9200",
      "elasticsearch-marvel-03:9200"]
```

7. Install Kibana and the Marvel Kibana plugin on `elasticsearch-marvel-01` using the instructions found in *Chapter 2, Installation and the Requirements for Elasticsearch*.

8. Configure the Marvel Kibana plugin by editing `config/kibana.yml` to look like this:

```
server.port: 5601

server.host: "0.0.0.0"

elasticsearch.url: http://elasticsearch-marvel-01:9200
```

9. Start Kibana on `elasticsearch-marvel-01` from the Kibana installation directory with the following command:

```
bin/kibana
```

The output from this command should look like this:

```
⬤ ⬤ ⬤                    ⇧ dnoble — elastic@elasticsearch-marvel-01: /opt/kibana/kibana-4.5.0-linux-x64 — ssh — 136×34
elastic@elasticsearch-marvel-01:/opt/kibana/kibana-4.5.0-linux-x64$ ./bin/kibana
  log   [21:16:40.816] [info][status][plugin:kibana] Status changed from uninitialized to green - Ready
  log   [21:16:40.858] [info][status][plugin:elasticsearch] Status changed from uninitialized to yellow - Waiting for Elasticsearch
  log   [21:16:40.862] [info][status][plugin:marvel] Status changed from uninitialized to yellow - Waiting for Elasticsearch
  log   [21:16:40.909] [info][status][plugin:kbn_vislib_vis_types] Status changed from uninitialized to green - Ready
  log   [21:16:40.925] [info][status][plugin:markdown_vis] Status changed from uninitialized to green - Ready
  log   [21:16:40.934] [info][status][plugin:metric_vis] Status changed from uninitialized to green - Ready
  log   [21:16:40.950] [info][status][plugin:spyModes] Status changed from uninitialized to green - Ready
  log   [21:16:41.165] [info][status][plugin:statusPage] Status changed from uninitialized to green - Ready
  log   [21:16:41.171] [info][status][plugin:table_vis] Status changed from uninitialized to green - Ready
  log   [21:16:41.208] [info][listening] Server running at http://0.0.0.0:5601
  log   [21:16:41.246] [info][status][plugin:elasticsearch] Status changed from yellow to green - Kibana index ready
  log   [21:16:41.366] [info][status][plugin:marvel] Status changed from yellow to green - Marvel index ready
```

10. Visit the Marvel dashboard on `elasticsearch-marvel-01` in a browser by going to `http://elasticsearch-marvel-01:5601/app/marvel`, as seen in the following screenshot:

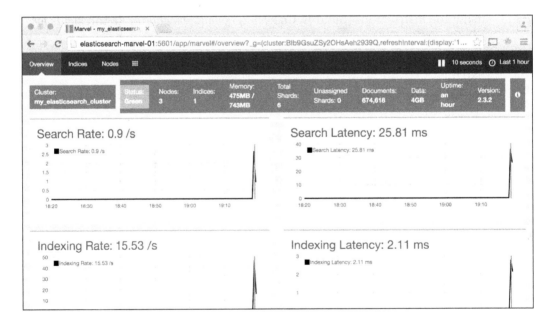

11. Scroll down the page and click the **Show History** or **Hide History** button (highlighted in the next screenshot) to view shard activity for the `twitter` index:

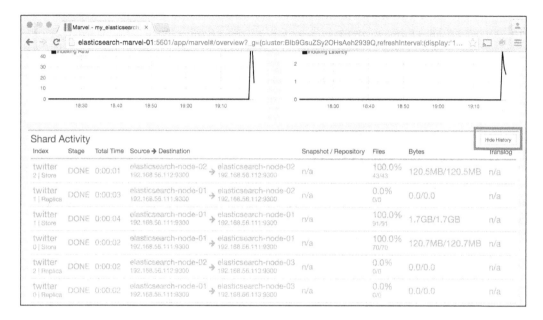

12. Open Elasticsearch-head on `elasticsearch-marvel-01` and view the indices automatically created by Marvel by visiting `http://elasticsearch-marvel-01:9200/_plugin/head/`:

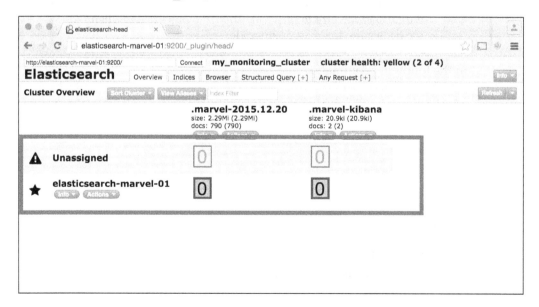

The `.marvel-2015.12.20` index contains historical data collected by Marvel. By default, Marvel creates one new index per day to store its data.

**Server time synchronization**

The clocks on all Elasticsearch hosts must be synchronized or Marvel won't show any data. Clock synchronization varies depending on server setup. On a cluster of Ubuntu hosts, run this command on all nodes to synchronize their clocks:

```
sudo ntpupdate pool.ntp.org
```

# Upgrading Marvel

Marvel can be upgraded on a rolling basis. This means that nodes are upgraded one at a time rather than having to shut down the entire cluster to perform an upgrade. For environments with a monitoring cluster and a production cluster, upgrade Marvel on the monitoring cluster before upgrading it on the production cluster.

To upgrade the Marvel Agent, run these steps on all nodes in the monitoring cluster (in this case, just `elasticsearch-marvel-01`), then for each node in the production cluster (`elasticsearch-node-01`, `elasticsearch-node-02`, and `elasticsearch-node-03`):

1. Optional: Disable shard allocation on all nodes.

Disabling shard allocation will make the upgrade faster because the cluster won't try to reallocate shards to other nodes when the node goes down for an upgrade.

Run the following command:

```
curl -XPUT elasticsearch-host-01:9200/_cluster/settings -d '{
    "transient" : {
        "cluster.routing.allocation.enable" : "none"
    }
}'
```

2. Stop Elasticsearch:

```
sudo /etc/init.d/elasticsearch stop
```

3. Remove the old Marvel plugin:

```
bin/plugin remove marvel-agent
```

4. Install the new Marvel plugin:

```
plugin install marvel-agent
```

5. Start Elasticsearch:

```
sudo /etc/init.d/elasticsearch start
```

6. Check logs for errors:

```
tail -f /var/log/elasticsearch/*
```

7. Once all nodes in the cluster are upgraded, re-enable shard allocation:

```
curl -XPUT elasticsearch-host-01:9200/_cluster/settings -d '{
    "transient" : {
        "cluster.routing.allocation.enable" : "all"
    }
}'
```

8. Repeat all of these steps for the production cluster.

   To upgrade the Marvel Kibana dashboard, run the following commands on `elasticsearch-marvel-01`

9. Uninstall the old Marvel Kibana plugin with the following command:

```
bin/kibana plugin --remove marvel
```

10. Install the new Marvel Kibana plugin. In this example, we are upgrading to Marvel 2.3.2:

```
bin/kibana plugin install marvel/2.3.2
```

# Configuring Marvel

This section covers how to configure the Marvel Agent and data index. Specifically, we cover:

- Setting the Marvel data store location
- Specifying which indices to monitor
- Security settings
- Data export frequency
- Marvel index configuration

# Marvel agent configuration settings

This section covers configuring the Marvel Agent. Configure the Agent by editing the `elasticsearch.yml` file on each node we are monitoring.

The `marvel.agent.exporters` setting determines where the Agent will deliver its metrics to. By default, the Marvel agent will export data to the same Elasticsearch instance that it is installed on. In our example cluster, we are exporting data to `elasticsearch-marvel-01`, and the configuration value looks like this:

```
marvel.agent.exporters:
  my_monitoring_cluster:
    type: http
    host: ["http://elasticsearch-marvel-01:9200"]
```

Other options for the `marvel.agent.exporters` settings include:

```
marvel.agent.exporters:
  your_exporter_name:
    type: http # Set to local or http
    host: [ "http://host-01:9200", "http://host-02:9200" ]
    # List of hosts to send data to over http or https

    auth:
      username: basic_auth_username # optional
      password: basic_auth_password # optional

    connection:
      timeout: 6s # optional: connection timeout
      read_timeout: 60s # optional: response timeout.
      keep_alive: true # persistent connections

    ssl:
      hostname_verification: true
        # https only: verify host certificate
      protocol: TLSv1.2 # https only: protocol
      truststore.path: /path/to/file # https only:
.jks truststore
      truststore.password: password
        # https only: .jks truststore password
      truststore.algorithm: SunX509
        # https only: .jks truststore algorithm

    index:
      name:
        time_format: YYYY.MM.dd
```

```
# marvel index suffix.
# Set to a value like YYYY.MM to create new
# indices monthly instead of daily
```

Other `elasticsearch.yml` configuration options are described here:

| Option | Default Value | Description |
|---|---|---|
| `marvel.enabled` | `true` | Controls whether monitoring data will be exported from this node. |
| `marvel.agent.interval` | `10s` | Time interval between monitoring data exports. Can be set to `-1` to disable exporting of data altogether. |
| `marvel.agent.indices` | `_all` List of | Indices to export data from. Supports wildcard *, addition +, and subtraction - operators. For example, to export data only from nodes that start with `twitter_`, except for the index `twitter_ development`, we would set this parameter to `+twitter_*,-twitter_ development`. |
| `marvel.agent.cluster. state.timeout` | `10m` | Timeout for collecting cluster state. |
| `marvel.agent.cluster. stats.timeout` | `10m` | Timeout for collecting cluster statistics. |
| `marvel.history.duration` | `7d` | Length of time to retain Marvel indices. The `marvel-agent` will automatically delete indices older than this value. Set to `-1` to disable automatic index deletion. |

After making any changes to `elasticsearch.yml`, restart Elasticsearch:

```
sudo /etc/init.d/elasticsearch restart
```

# Marvel index configuration

This section covers how to configure the number of shards, replicas, and various other index settings used by Marvel. By default, each Marvel index uses one shard and one replica:

1.  To view the default settings used by Marvel, run:

    ```
    curl -XGET
      "http://elasticsearch-marvel-01:9200/_template/marvel?pretty"
    ```

This will return a large JSON object. The settings that are important are `marvel.order`, `marvel.template`, and `marvel.settings`:

```
{
  "marvel" : {
    "order" : 0,
    "template" : ".marvel*",
    "settings" : {
      "index.mapper.dynamic" : "true",
      "index.marvel.index_format" : "6",
      "index.analysis.analyzer.default.type" : "standard",
      "index.number_of_replicas" : "1",
      "index.number_of_shards" : "1",
      "index.analysis.analyzer.default.stopwords" : "_none_"
    },
    ...
}
```

2. For large Marvel clusters, consider increasing the number of shards to no more than the number of hosts in your cluster for optimal performance. For example, for a four-node Marvel monitoring cluster, increase the number of shards to four with the following command:

```
curl -XPOST
  "http://elasticsearch-marvel-01:9200/_template/
  marvel_01?pretty" -d '{
    "template": ".marvel*",
    "order": 1,
    "settings": {
        "number_of_shards": 4
    }
}'
```

Notice the template is set to `.marvel*` in order to only alter Marvel's indices. Additionally, the `order` setting is 1 so this template, `marvel_01`, will have higher precedence than the default template `marvel`.

Now, when checking the Marvel settings, we should see:

```
curl -XGET
  "http://elasticsearch-marvel-01:9200/_template/marvel_01?pretty"
{
  "marvel_01" : {
    "order" : 1,
    "template" : ".marvel*",
    "settings" : {
      "index.number_of_shards" : "4"
    },
    "mappings" : { },
    "aliases" : { }
  }
}
```

# Understanding the Marvel dashboard

This section covers how to use the Marvel dashboard to better understand the state of your cluster.

To make monitoring our cluster more interesting, we'll stream more Twitter data into it using the `stream2es` program, and run random queries against the index using a custom bash script described in this section.

See *Chapter 3, Elasticsearch-head and Bigdesk* for detailed instructions on how to install and use `stream2es`, but, for quick reference, start `stream2es` using the following command:

```
./stream2es twitter --target
  http://elasticsearch-node-01:9200/twitter/status
```

Next, we'll simulate user interactions by running random queries against the `twitter` index. Create a new bash script called `run_queries.sh` with the following content:

```
#!/bin/sh

# Path to dictionary file
DICTIONARY_PATH=/usr/share/dict/words
ELASTICSEARCH_URI=http://elasticsearch-node-01:9200/twitter

# Total dictionary words
```

```
TOTAL_WORDS=`wc -l $DICTIONARY_PATH | awk '{print $1}'`

while :
do
    # Pick a random word
    WORD_INDEX=`python
      -c "import random;print random.randint(1,$TOTAL_WORDS)"`
    WORD=`sed "${WORD_INDEX}q;d" $DICTIONARY_PATH`

    # Run query
    echo "Querying elasticsearch $ELASTICSEARCH_URI for $WORD "
    curl -XGET "${ELASTICSEARCH_URI}/_search?q=$WORD"

    # Sleep for one second before running the next query
    echo
    echo "Press [CTRL+C] to stop.."
    sleep 1
done
```

This script queries the Elasticsearch `twitter` index with a random dictionary word once every second.

You may need to install a dictionary on some Linux systems to get this to work. On Ubuntu, to get a dictionary of American English or British English words, run the following.

For American English:

**sudo apt-get install wamerican**

For British English:

**sudo apt-get install wbritish**

Now make the run_queries.sh script executable:

**chmod +x run_queries.sh**

And finally, run the run_queries.sh script to start hitting our cluster with random queries once a second:

**./run_queries.sh**

After running `stream2es` and `run_queries.sh` for a few minutes, open Marvel and navigate to the Overview dashboard to explore the impact of these scripts on our cluster.

# Overview dashboard

The **Overview** dashboard is the landing page of the Marvel Kibana dashboard. After running the `stream2es` command and `run_queries.sh` script mentioned previously for a few minutes, this dashboard will look something like this:

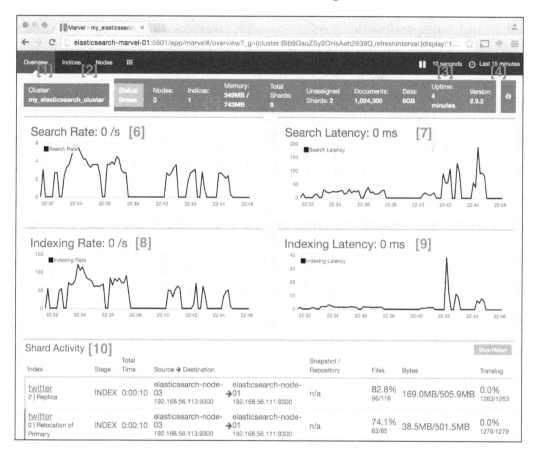

Here are the labels from the previous screenshot:

| No. | Description |
|---|---|
| 1 | Dashboard title. |
| 2 | Other Marvel dashboards. |
| 3 | Page auto-refresh interval. |
| 4 | Time filter. Defaults to **Last 1 hour**. |
| 5 | Cluster information including cluster status, number of nodes, total memory, and number of documents. |
| 6 | Current and historical search rate. Sample use case: see how heavy search traffic affects the cluster. |
| 7 | Current and historical search latency. Sample use case: diagnose why queries are running slow. |
| 8 | Current and historical indexing rate. Sample use case: diagnose why a bulk index operation failed. |
| 9 | Current and historical indexing latency. Sample use case: diagnose why indexing operations are slow. |
| 10 | Shard activity. Gives the status of shards when they are recovering. |

Note that `run_queries.sh` only runs one query per second, but the **Search Request Rate** chart shows an average of about three queries per second. This is because every time a query is run, it's actually being run against all three data nodes. The **Search Request Rate** chart shows the average queries per second across all data nodes.

Any of Marvel's charts can be filtered by time range by clicking and dragging on the chart, shown in the following figure:

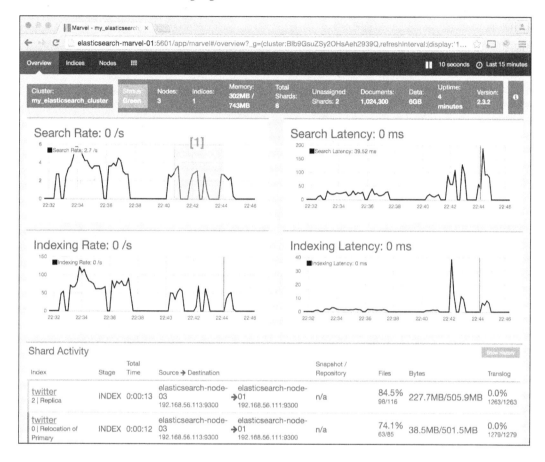

Here is the label from the previous screenshot:

| Number | Description |
|--------|-------------|
| 1 | Click and drag on any chart to filter the chart by time. |

After applying a filter, the Marvel charts and cluster information banner will update to show the state of the cluster at the selected moment in time. In the following screenshot, we can see that the cluster was in a `yellow` state during the selected time period:

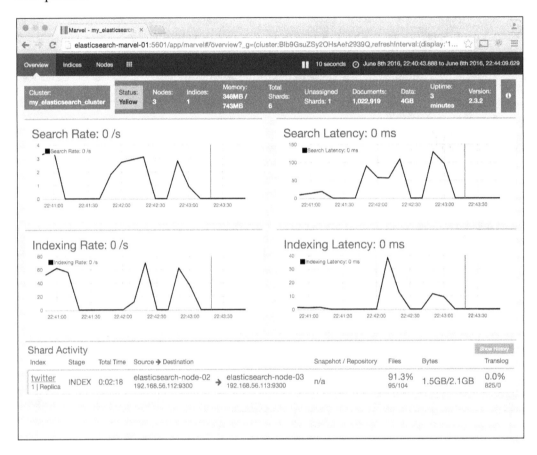

# Indices dashboard

The **Indices** dashboard lets you examine historical data for a specific index, including:

- Search rate
- Index rate
- Index size
- Memory
- Document count
- Field data size

The **Indices** dashboard is very similar to the **Overview** dashboard, except for the list of indices at the bottom of the page, as seen in the following screenshot:

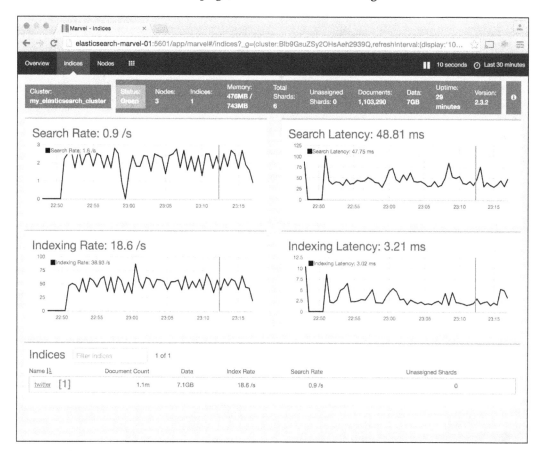

Here is the label from the preceding screenshot:

| Number | Description |
|--------|-------------|
| 1 | List of all indices in the cluster. |

Click on the `twitter` index at the bottom of this page to bring us to a page showing historical and real-time metrics for that particular index:

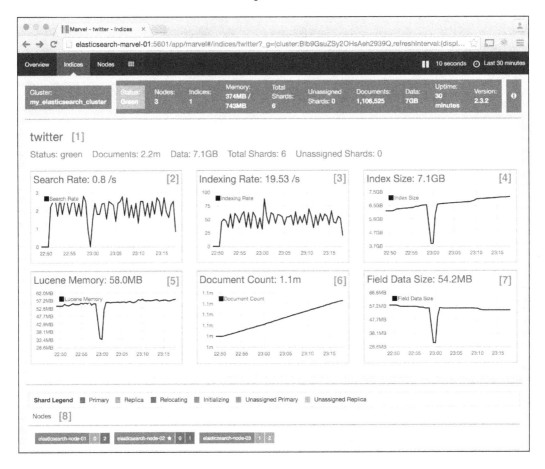

Here are the labels from the previous screenshot:

| Number | Description |
|---|---|
| 1 | Index details. |
| 2 | Historical and real-time search rate for the index. |
| 3 | Historical and real-time indexing rate. |
| 4 | Historical and real-time index size. |
| 5 | Historical and real-time Lucene memory size. |
| 6 | Historical and real-time document count. |

| Number | Description |
|--------|-------------|
| 7 | Historical and real-time field data size. Sample use case: diagnose `OutOfMemoryError` exceptions. |
| 8 | Shard distribution for this index. Click on any of the nodes to go to the node details page, described in the next section. |

# Nodes dashboard

The **Nodes** dashboard provides an overview of the cluster's health and node utilization, in addition to historical and real-time statistics for specific nodes. This dashboard is used to examine Elasticsearch issues such as:

- Nodes in the cluster that are down
- Nodes that are running low on disk space
- Nodes with high CPU and memory usage

Opening the **Nodes** dashboard brings us to the following page:

This screenshot shows an overview of all nodes in the cluster, along with some real-time metrics. One advantage this page has over Elasticsearch-head is that if a node goes down, this page will identify that the node used to be part of the cluster but is currently offline. Elasticsearch-head on the other hand won't display the offline node at all.

Clicking on a specific node opens up a dashboard showing data only for that host. The next screenshot shows the node stats for `elasticsearch-node-02`:

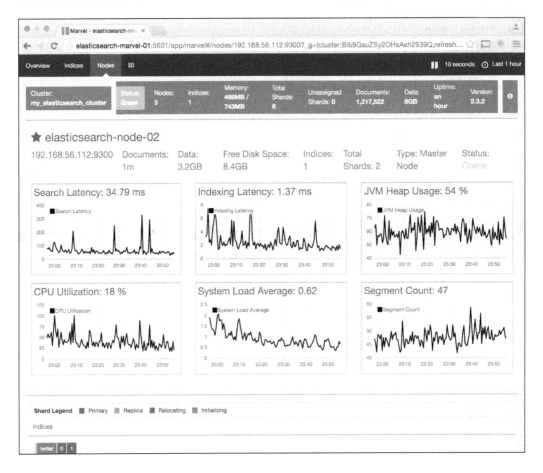

This page shows several historical and real-time metrics for the selected node:

- **Search Latency**: Historical analysis of search performance.

- **Index Latency**: Historical analysis of data index performance.

- **JVM Heap Usage**: High heap usage may indicate Java `OutOfMemoryError` exceptions.

- **CPU Utilization**: High CPU utilization can be caused by a number of factors, but some common causes are running complex queries and shard movement.

- **System Load Average**: This metric is a measure of the average amount of work performed by the node. This value should ideally be less than the number of CPU cores on the node.

- **Segment Count**: Number of Lucene segments. This statistic will vary from cluster to cluster, but if the value increases to higher than usual, try running a cluster optimization.

- **Shard Legend**: Shows what shards are allocated to this node.

# Monitoring node failures

As mentioned previously, Marvel keeps track of nodes even after they leave the cluster. This is useful when working with large clusters that have many nodes to keep track of.

We will demonstrate how the Marvel **Nodes** dashboard displays node failures by shutting down `elasticsearch-node-01`:

```
# From elasticsearch-node-01
sudo service elasticsearch stop
```

The **Nodes** dashboard in Marvel now looks like this:

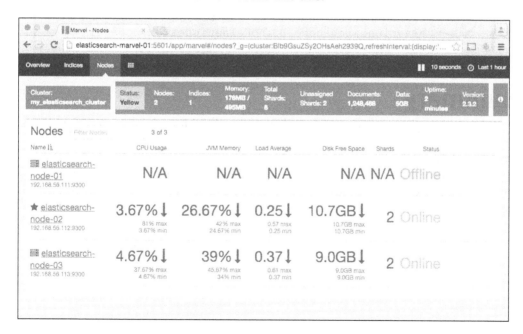

Here we can see Marvel indicates `elasticsearch-node-01` used to be part of the cluster, but is currently offline.

Elasticsearch-head, on the other hand, shows us the cluster in a `yellow` state, but does not indicate that `elasticsearch-node-01` was ever part of the cluster:

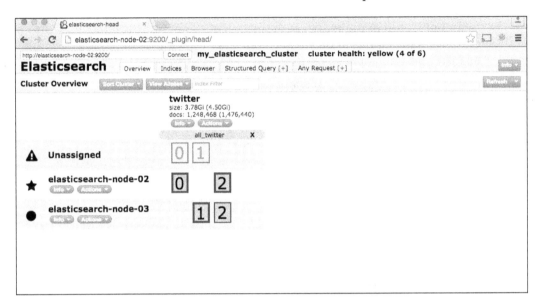

 Elasticsearch-head only displays `elasticsearch-node-02` and `elasticsearch-node-03`, not `elasticsearch-node-01`.

# Summary

This chapter covered how to install and configure the Marvel Agent and the Marvel Kibana dashboard. Additionally, it covered setting up a secondary monitoring cluster for Marvel to store its metrics. Finally, the chapter talked about the various Marvel Kibana dashboard pages and discussed at a high level how to use those pages to diagnose cluster issues. The next chapter talks about another monitoring tool, Kopf, and goes into more detail about how to use Kibana.

# System Monitoring

**5**

The previous two chapters focused on Elasticsearch monitoring tools, including Elasticsearch-head, Bigdesk, and Marvel. This chapter will introduce another monitoring tool, **Kopf**. We will also discuss **Elasticsearch, Logstash, and Kibana (ELK)**, Nagios, and various GNU/Linux command line tools in terms of general purpose system monitoring.

This chapter covers these topics:

- Monitoring Elasticsearch with Kopf
- Configuring an Elasticsearch, Logstash, and Kibana (ELK) stack for system log file aggregation and analysis
- System-level monitoring of a cluster using Nagios
- GNU/Linux command line tools for system and process management

## Working with Kopf

Kopf is a web-based cluster management tool like Elasticsearch-head, but has a more modern look and a few different features. With Kopf, users can check the state of nodes and indices, run REST queries, and perform basic management tasks.

# Installing Kopf

Kopf works on Elasticsearch 0.90.x and up. Use the following table to determine which Kopf version is best suited to your cluster:

| Elasticsearch Version | Kopf Branch |
| --- | --- |
| 0.90.x | 0.90 |
| 1.x | 1.0 |
| 2.x | 2.0 |

To install Kopf, follow these steps:

1.  Install Kopf on at least one node in your cluster as an Elasticsearch plugin with the following command, replacing {branch} with the value from the branch column in the preceding table:

    ```
    $ sudo /usr/share/elasticsearch/bin/plugin install lmenezes/
    elasticsearch-kopf/{branch}
    ```

    This example will install Kopf on elasticsearch-node-01. Since this node is running Elasticsearch 2.3.2, the command will look like this:

    ```
    $ sudo /usr/share/elasticsearch/bin/plugin install lmenezes/
    elasticsearch-kopf/2.0
    ```

2.  To open Kopf, browse to:

    ```
    http://elasticsearch-node-01:9200/_plugin/kopf/
    ```

    You should see something like this:

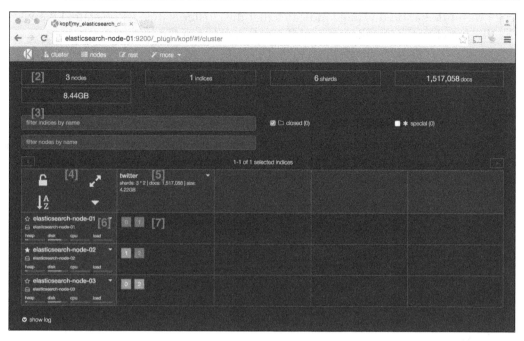

Kopf cluster page

| No. | Description |
| --- | --- |
| 1 | Titlebar and cluster state |
| 2 | Cluster summary |
| 3 | Display filters |
| 4 | Node and index actions |
| 5 | Indices |
| 6 | Nodes |
| 7 | Shard allocations |

The green title bar on this page indicates that the cluster is in a green state. Likewise, the title bar changes to yellow or red if it enters either of those states.

All Kopf dashboard pages also show the indicators listed on the top of this screenshot, including number of nodes, indices, shards, documents, and total index size.

# The cluster page

The screenshot in the previous section shows the Kopf cluster page. The Elasticsearch cluster's nodes, indices, and shard allocations are listed on this page. This page also provides the following administrative capabilities:

- Closing and opening indices
- Optimizing indices
- Refreshing indices
- Clearing index caches
- Deleting indices
- Disabling/enabling shard allocation
- Viewing index settings
- Viewing index mappings

Like the **Cluster Overview** tab in Elasticsearch-head, the Kopf **cluster** page is a great first stop when diagnosing Elasticsearch issues. It will inform you of the cluster state, whether a node is down, and if the node has a high heap/disk/CPU/load.

# The nodes page

The **nodes** page, shown in the following screenshot, provides figures for load, CPU usage, JVM heap usage, disk usage, and uptime for all nodes in the cluster:

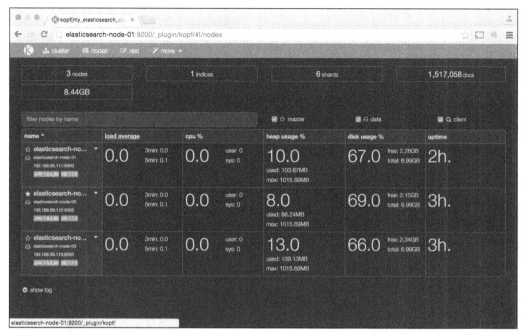

Kopf nodes page

This page, like the **cluster** page, is a good starting point when diagnosing Elasticsearch issues.

# The rest page

The Kopf **rest** page is a general-purpose tool for running arbitrary queries against Elasticsearch. You can run any query in the Elasticsearch API using this page. The following screenshot is running a simple **Search API** query against the Elasticsearch cluster:

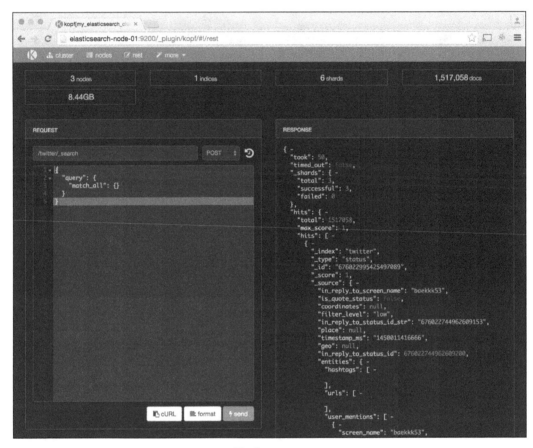

Kopf rest page

The **rest** page is useful for everything from testing query syntax to retrieving cluster metrics, and can help in gauging and optimizing query performance. For example, if a particular query is running slowly, use the **rest** page to test different variations of the query and determine which query components have the highest performance impact.

# The more dropdown

The **more** dropdown has a variety of other cluster management tools, including:

| Tool Name | Description |
|---|---|
| Create Index | Create an index and assign a number of shards, replicas, mapping, and other settings |
| Cluster Settings | Configure cluster, routing, and recovery settings |
| Aliases | View existing and create new index aliases |
| Analysis | Test and verify index analyzers |
| Percolator | View existing and create new percolator queries |
| Warmers | View existing and create new index warmer queries |
| Snapshot | Create new index snapshots on the local filesystem, URL, S3, HDFS, or Azure |
| Index Templates | View existing and create new index templates |
| Cat APIs | Run a subset of all possible Elasticsearch API "Cat" methods |
| Hot Threads | Query for Elasticsearch "Hot" threads |

The following screenshot shows the **HOT THREADS** page. This page is helpful when diagnosing slow search and indexing performance:

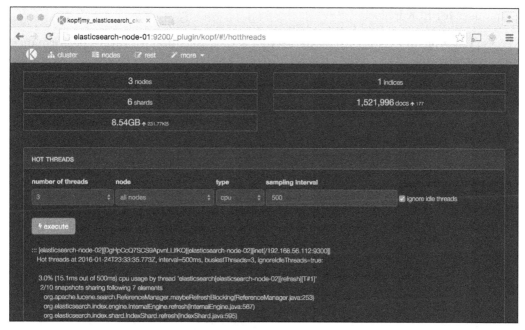

Hot Threads

# Working with Logstash and Kibana

Logstash is a utility for aggregating and normalizing log files from disparate sources and storing them in an Elasticsearch cluster. Once logs are stored in Elasticsearch, we will use Kibana, the same tool Marvel's user interface is built on, to view and explore our aggregated logs.

# ELK

The Elasticsearch community refers to the Elasticsearch, Logstash, and Kibana tool combination as the ELK stack. This section shows how to load NGINX server logs into ELK, but there are many other potential use cases for these technologies.

ELK can help us explore NGINX server logs by:

- Visualizing server traffic over time
- Plotting server visits by location on a map
- Searching logs by resource extension (HTML, JS, CSS, and so on), IP address, byte count, or user-agent strings
- Discovering web requests that result in internal server errors
- Finding attackers in a distributed denial of service attack

Other uses for ELK include:

- Logging all Elasticsearch queries in a web application for future performance analysis
- Aggregating server system logs into one location for analysis and visualization
- Logging operations from a data processing or ingestion pipeline for future analysis and auditing

# Installation

Although this example will store aggregate log data from Logstash directly into Elasticsearch, it's important to ensure that these aggregated logs do not affect the performance of the production cluster. To avoid this potential performance problem, we'll configure Logstash to route logs to a secondary monitoring cluster; in our case, this is the `elasticsearch-marvel-01` node.

# Installing Logstash

It doesn't matter what host Logstash lives on, since it can redirect logs to any Elasticsearch instance. Since Kibana will be installed on `elasticsearch-marvel-01`, we'll put Logstash there as well:

From `elasticsearch-marvel-01`, run the following:

```
sudo mkdir /opt/logstash

sudo chown -R `whoami` /opt/logstash

cd /opt/logstash

wget https://download.elastic.co/
  logstash/logstash/logstash-2.1.1.tar.gz

tar xzvf logstash-2.1.1.tar.gz

cd logstash-2.1.1/
```

# Loading NGINX logs

Now let's load some sample NGINX logs into Elasticsearch using Logstash. While Logstash has built-in parsers for many different log types (Apache, Linux syslogs, and so on), it doesn't natively support NGINX logs. This means that users have to explicitly tell Logstash how to deal with these files. To address this, follow these steps:

1. Put some sample NGINX log files in `/opt/logstash/logs`:

   ```
   $ ls -1 /opt/logstash/logs | head -n20
   ```

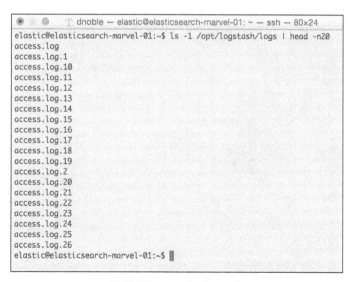

NGINX log files for Logstash

2.  Create a new file on /opt/logstash/patterns/nginx.grok on
    elasticsearch-marvel-01 with the following content:

```
NGINXACCESS
  %{IPORHOST:remote_addr} -
  %{USERNAME:remote_user} \[
  %{HTTPDATE:timestamp}\]
  %{QS:request} %{INT:status}
  %{INT:body_bytes_sent}
  %{QS:http_referer}
  %{QS:http_user_agent}
```

Then create a Logstash configuration file at /opt/logstash/logstash.conf
with the following content:

```
input {
  file {
    type => "nginx"
    path => "/opt/logstash/logs/access.log*"
    start_position => "beginning"
    sincedb_path => "/dev/null"
  }
}

filter {
  if [type] == "nginx" {
  grok {
    patterns_dir => "./patterns"
    match => {
        "message" => "%{NGINXACCESS}"
    }
  }
  date {
    match => [ "timestamp" , "dd/MMM/yyyy:HH:mm:ss Z" ]
  }
  geoip {
    source => "remote_addr"
  }

  }
}

output {
  elasticsearch { hosts => ["elasticsearch-marvel-01:9200"] }
}
```

This configuration tells Logstash to read all `access.log*` files from the filesystem using our newly defined `nginx` format, identifies the timestamp column used by our NGINX format, tells Logstash to use a Geo IP lookup on the visitor's IP address, and finally tells Logstash to save logs to the Elasticsearch host instance at `elasticsearch-marvel-01:9200`.

 Read more about the Logstash configuration file format at: `https://www.elastic.co/guide/en/logstash/current/configuration.html`.

3. Now run Logstash, specifying the configuration file:

```
cd /opt/logstash

./logstash-2.1.1/bin/logstash agent -f logstash.conf
```

After a few minutes, Logstash will load all of the data into Elasticsearch. The new index created in Kopf should now be viewable.

The next section will focus on exploring the data in Kibana.

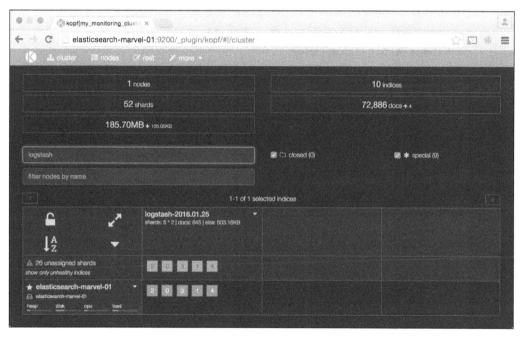

Viewing Logstash index from Kopf

This process will go much faster if the `geoip` configuration setting from the `logstash.conf` configuration file is removed.

## Installing Kibana

Follow these steps to install Kibana on your system:

1.  Determine the appropriate version of Kibana to download from `https://www.elastic.co/downloads/kibana`. Since this example is using Elasticsearch 2.3.2, we'll install Kibana 4.5.4.

2.  Download and unpackage Kibana on `elasticsearch-marvel-01` in the `/opt/kibana/` directory:

    ```
    sudo mkdir /opt/kibana

    sudo chown -R `whoami` /opt/kibana/

    cd /opt/kibana/

    wget https://download.elastic.co/
      kibana/kibana/kibana-4.5.0-linux-x64.tar.gz

    tar xzvf kibana-4.5.0-linux-x64.tar.gz

    cd kibana-4.5.0-linux-x64/
    ```

3.  Edit Kibana's `conf/kibana.yml` file to point to the correct Elasticsearch host. In this case, change this:

    ```
    # The Elasticsearch instance to use for all your queries.
    elasticsearch_url: "http://localhost:9200"
    ```

    To:

    ```
    # The Elasticsearch instance to use for all your queries.
    elasticsearch_url: "http://elasticsearch-marvel-01:9200"
    ```

4. Now start Kibana:

   `./bin/kibana`

5. Visit `http://elasticsearch-marvel-01:5601/` to view the Kibana landing page. It should look like the following screenshot:

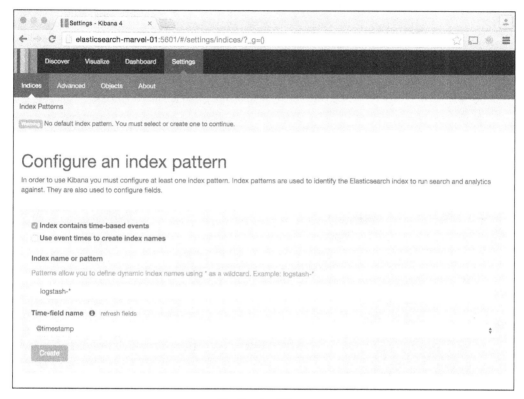

Configuring Kibana

6. Notice `logstash-*` is already selected by default, so just click the **Create** button to continue.

7.  Navigate to the **Discover** tab to start exploring your log data:

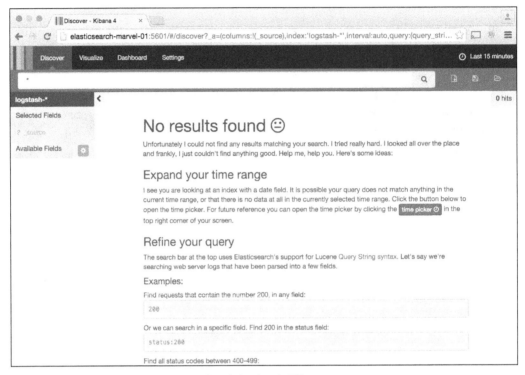

Search for data in Kibana

You may not see any data here at first. This is because all of the data loaded is more than 15 minutes old.

8. Click the date range filter in the upper-right of the page, by default set to **Last 15 Minutes**. Now select a more appropriate range, such as **This Month**. You should now start to see some results:

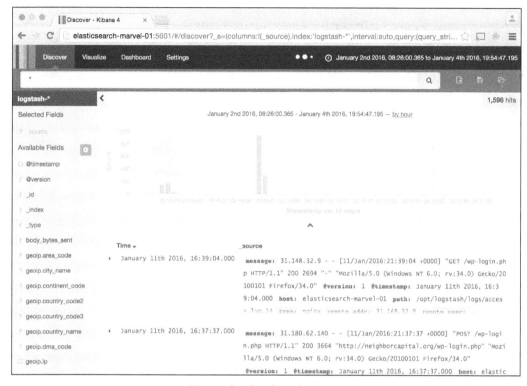

Viewing log data from this month

The default `_source` column is a little hard to read, so specify some columns from the left-hand side of the page: `http_user_agent`, `remote_addr`, and `status`. Clicking on any of these selected columns will run an aggregation query displaying the most commonly occurring values for each field:

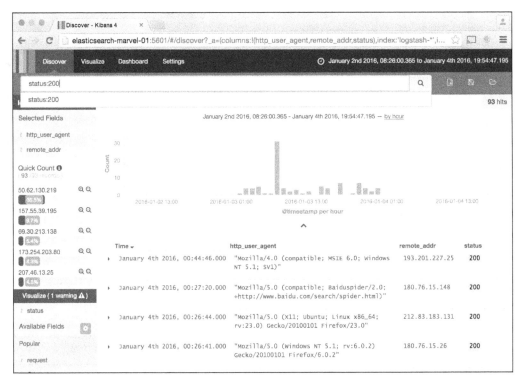

Applying search filters to Kibana results

The **Visualize** page lets us create arbitrary data visualizations. As an example, we'll create two sample visualizations: a Tile map to plot the geolocated IP addresses in our dataset, and a Vertical bar chart for displaying counts of different HTTP status codes in the log files. Follow these steps:

1. First, configure the Tile map visualization as shown here:

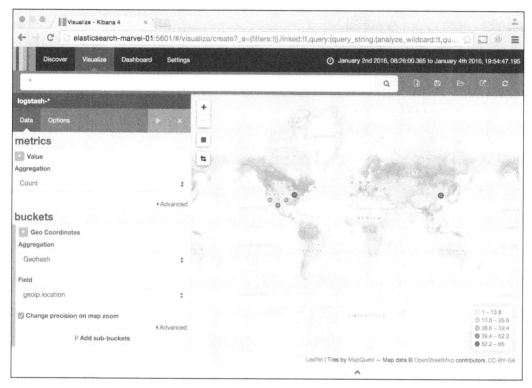

Geospatial visualization of Kibana results

2. Click **Save** to save your changes, and create the Vertical bar chart:

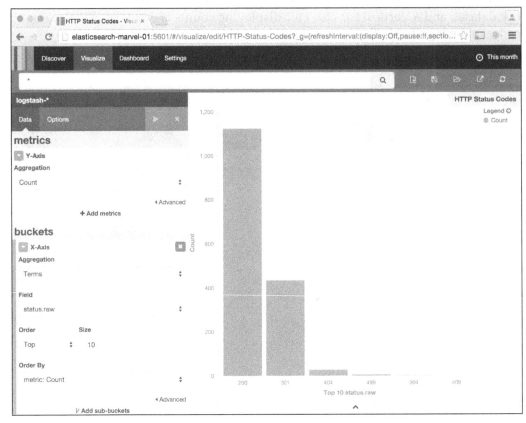

Breakdown by HTTP status code

3. After saving this chart, go to the **Dashboard** page in order to display both components on the same page.

4. Select the two components by clicking the **Add Visualization** button. Move them around the dashboard to resize and reorder them until you get something like this:

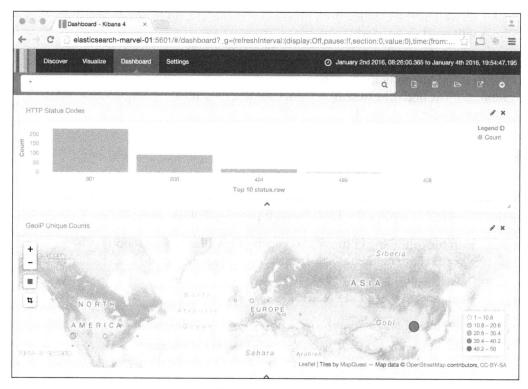

Kibana dashboard view

Learn more about Kibana and Logstash by visiting the official Elasticsearch documentation at:

- `https://www.elastic.co/videos/kibana-logstash`
- `https://www.elastic.co/products/kibana`
- `https://www.elastic.co/products/logstash`

# Working with Nagios

Nagios is a system monitoring and alerting tool. This section will focus on configuring a simple Nagios installation that monitors the nodes in our Elasticsearch cluster, as well as the Elasticsearch process on those. If a node or process shuts down, Nagios will send us an alert.

It's a good idea to install Nagios on a host outside of the Elasticsearch clusters in order to avoid affecting the monitoring process due to other things going on in the system, such as high Elasticsearch load. Create a new host for Nagios and call it `elasticsearch-nagios-01`.

## Installing Nagios

In addition to the dedicated Nagios host, `elasticsearch-nagios-01`, install the **Nagios Remote Plugin Executor** (**NRPE**) server on all of the Elasticsearch cluster nodes in order to monitor the Elasticsearch process. Follow these steps:

1. Run the following command on each of the Elasticsearch nodes: `elasticsearch-node-01`, `elasticsearch-node-02`, `elasticsearch-node-03`, and `elasticsearch-marvel-01`:

   ```
   sudo apt-get install nagios-nrpe-server
   ```

2. Then install Nagios on the new host `elasticsearch-nagios-01`:

   ```
   sudo apt-get install nagios3 nagios-nrpe-plugin
   ```

3. This process will ask you to enter a password. Make sure you remember it.

   Now a Nagios plugin is needed to ensure that Elasticsearch is running. There are several plugins available, but this book uses a simple script available on GitHub: `https://github.com/orthecreedence/check_elasticsearch`.

4. To download and install this script on `elasticsearch-nagios-01`, run:

   ```
   wget
     https://raw.githubusercontent.com/orthecreedence/
     check_elasticsearch/master/check_elasticsearch

   chmod +x check_elasticsearch

   sudo cp check_elasticsearch /usr/lib/nagios/plugins/
   ```

5. Next, add a Nagios command to run this plugin. On `elasticsearch-nagios-01`, create a new file, `/etc/nagios-plugins/config/elasticsearch.cfg`, with this content:

   ```
   # Check to ensure elasticsearch is running
   define command{
   ```

```
        command_name      check_elasticsearch
        command_line      /usr/lib/nagios/plugins/check_
elasticsearch -H $HOSTNAME$ -P 9200
        }
```

6.  Lastly, specify which hosts to monitor for the Nagios server. Be sure to have it monitor the Elasticsearch process on those hosts, using the `check_elasticsearch` utility, by editing the configuration file `/etc/nagios3/conf.d/localhost_nagios2.cfg`:

```
define host{
        use                     generic-host
        host_name               elasticsearch-node-01
        alias                   elasticsearch-node-01
        address                 192.168.56.111
        }

define host{
        use                     generic-host
        host_name               elasticsearch-node-02
        alias                   elasticsearch-node-02
        address                 192.168.56.112
        }

define host{
        use                     generic-host
        host_name               elasticsearch-node-03
        alias                   elasticsearch-node-03
        address                 192.168.56.113
        }

define host{
        use                     generic-host
        host_name               elasticsearch-marvel-01
        alias                   elasticsearch-marvel-01
        address                 192.168.56.120
        }

define hostgroup {
        hostgroup_name   elasticsearch-servers
                alias           Elasticsearch servers
                members         elasticsearch-node-01,
                    elasticsearch-node-02,
                    elasticsearch-node-03,
                    elasticsearch-marvel-01
        }
```

```
define contact{
        contact_name Elasticsearch Admin
        service_notification_period 24x7
        host_notification_period 24x7
        service_notification_options w,u,c,r,f
        host_notification_options d,u,r,f
        service_notification_commands
          notify-service-by-email
        host_notification_commands notify-host-by-email
        email admin@your-domain.com
        }

define service{
        use
          generic-service            ;
          Name of service template to use
        hostgroup_name
          elasticsearch-servers
        service_description              Elasticsearch
        check_command                    check_elasticsearch
        }
```

7.  Next, configure `elasticsearch-node-01`, `elasticsearch-node-02`, `elasticsearch-node-03`, and `elasticsearch-marvel-01` to allow our Nagios host `elasticsearch-nagios-01` to collect metrics:

    **`sudo vim /etc/nagios/nrpe.cfg`**

8.  Edit the `allowed_hosts` setting to include the `elasticsearch-nagios-01` IP address; in our case, this is `192.168.56.130`:

    **`allowed_hosts=127.0.0.1,192.168.56.130`**

9.  Now restart the NRPE server on all nodes in our Elasticsearch clusters:

    **`sudo service nagios-nrpe-server restart`**

10. And finally, restart `nagios3` on `elasticsearch-nagios-01`:

    **`sudo service nagios3 restart`**

11. Open a web browser to see the Nagios web administration portal, with the username `nagiosadmin` and the password you entered earlier:

    `http://elasticsearch-nagios-01/nagios3`

12. After giving Nagios a few minutes to collect metrics on all nodes, click on the **Hosts** sidebar link to see the state of all nodes in the clusters:

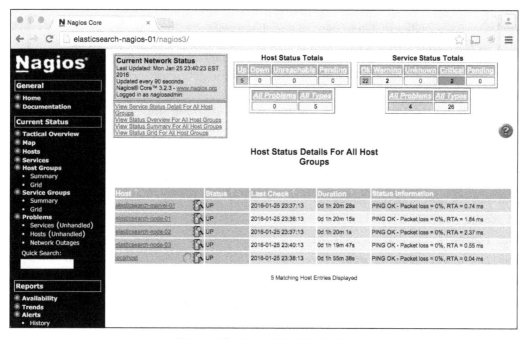

Viewing Elasticsearch hosts in Nagios

13. Click **Services** in the left-hand menu to see the state of the Elasticsearch process on each node:

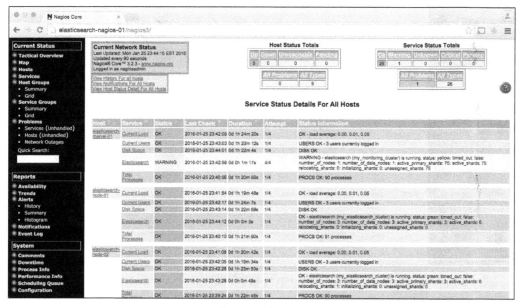

Viewing Elasticsearch status in Nagios

Notice that in `elasticsearch-marvel-01`, the Elasticsearch process is in a yellow **WARNING** state. This means that the cluster is in a `yellow` state, because there is only one node in the Marvel cluster and not all shards are replicated.

Now we'll demonstrate what Nagios does when one node shuts down and we stop the Elasticsearch process on a different node.

Shut down `elasticsearch-node-01` and disable Elasticsearch on `elasticsearch-node-02`:

```
ssh root@elasticsearch-node-01
shutdown -h now
ssh root@elasticsearch-node-02
service elasticsearch stop
```

The next time Nagios polls for the cluster state (this will take a few minutes), the following will display on the Nagios web dashboard's services page:

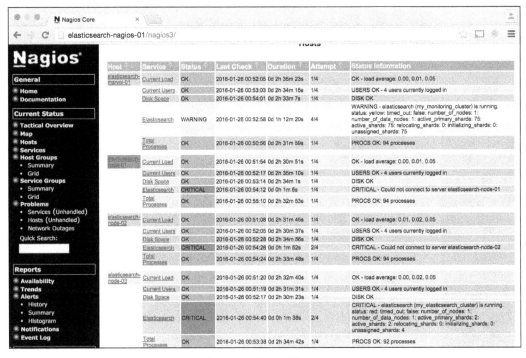

Error reporting in Nagios

Nagios now indicates that `elasticsearch-node-01` is down and that it can't connect to the Elasticsearch process on `elasticsearch-node-02`. Nagios also indicates Elasticsearch has entered a `red` state on `elasticsearch-node-03` because not all shards are available. Nagios will send `admin@your-domain.com` an email about the warnings and errors, based on our previous configuration. Things will return to normal after starting `elasticsearch-node-01` and restarting Elasticsearch on `elasticsearch-node-02`.

# Command line tools for system and process management

The command line is an invaluable tool for system monitoring. In this section, we'll go over a few basic GNU/Linux command line utilities for system and process management. Knowing these tools is essential for anyone managing an Elasticsearch cluster on GNU/Linux.

## top

The `top` command lists processes with the highest CPU and memory. This tool is useful to determine whether a process other than Elasticsearch is hogging resources, or to check whether Elasticsearch is using an abnormal amount of CPU or memory.

The `top` command refreshes automatically, so you only have to run it once and watch.

When running the command, you should see the following result:

```
●  ● ⬆ dnoble — elastic@elasticsearch-node-01: /home/humangeo — ssh — 80×24
top - 00:57:49 up  4:12,  3 users,  load average: 0.03, 0.04, 0.05
Tasks:  84 total,   1 running,  83 sleeping,   0 stopped,   0 zombie
Cpu(s):  0.3%us,  0.7%sy,  0.0%ni, 99.0%id,  0.0%wa,  0.0%hi,  0.0%si,  0.0%st
Mem:    502636k total,   496736k used,     5900k free,     9636k buffers
Swap:   520188k total,     3364k used,   516824k free,   103012k cached

  PID USER      PR  NI  VIRT  RES  SHR S %CPU %MEM    TIME+  COMMAND
 2501 elastics  20   0 3064m 315m  27m S  1.3 64.3  1:45.10 java
    1 root      20   0 24332 1920 1328 S  0.0  0.4  0:00.60 init
    2 root      20   0     0    0    0 S  0.0  0.0  0:00.00 kthreadd
    3 root      20   0     0    0    0 S  0.0  0.0  0:01.88 ksoftirqd/0
    5 root       0 -20     0    0    0 S  0.0  0.0  0:00.00 kworker/0:0H
    7 root       0 -20     0    0    0 S  0.0  0.0  0:00.00 kworker/u:0H
    8 root      RT   0     0    0    0 S  0.0  0.0  0:00.00 migration/0
    9 root      20   0     0    0    0 S  0.0  0.0  0:00.00 rcu_bh
   10 root      20   0     0    0    0 S  0.0  0.0  0:02.55 rcu_sched
   11 root      RT   0     0    0    0 S  0.0  0.0  0:00.26 watchdog/0
   12 root       0 -20     0    0    0 S  0.0  0.0  0:00.00 cpuset
   13 root       0 -20     0    0    0 S  0.0  0.0  0:00.00 khelper
   14 root      20   0     0    0    0 S  0.0  0.0  0:00.00 kdevtmpfs
   15 root       0 -20     0    0    0 S  0.0  0.0  0:00.00 netns
   16 root      20   0     0    0    0 S  0.0  0.0  0:00.00 bdi-default
   17 root       0 -20     0    0    0 S  0.0  0.0  0:00.00 kintegrityd
   18 root       0 -20     0    0    0 S  0.0  0.0  0:00.00 kblockd
```

The top command

Press *Shift+M* while `top` is running to sort processes by those using the most memory instead of CPU.

# tail

The `tail -f` command is useful for viewing log files in real time. Use it to view Elasticsearch log files as follows:

```
tail -f /var/log/elasticsearch/*
```

```
● ● ●        ⬆ dnoble — elastic@elasticsearch-node-01: ~ — ssh — 80×24
.java:617)
        at java.lang.Thread.run(Thread.java:745)
[2016-06-10 01:01:37,865][INFO ][cluster.routing.allocation] [elasticsearch-node
-01] Cluster health status changed from [YELLOW] to [RED] (reason: [nodes joined
]).
[2016-06-10 01:01:37,870][INFO ][cluster.service         ] [elasticsearch-node-
01] new_master {elasticsearch-node-01}{x1gBdnHhSnuiSLyN-n3tEA}{192.168.56.111}{1
92.168.56.111:9300}, reason: zen-disco-join(elected_as_master, [0] joins receive
d)
[2016-06-10 01:01:37,872][INFO ][cluster.routing         ] [elasticsearch-node-
01] delaying allocation for [3] unassigned shards, next check in [54.5s]
[2016-06-10 01:01:47,213][INFO ][cluster.service         ] [elasticsearch-node-
01] added {{elasticsearch-node-03}{90xMsoiDQWmwhKkqsaf-Ww}{192.168.56.113}{192.1
68.56.113:9300},}, reason: zen-disco-join(join from node[{elasticsearch-node-03}
{90xMsoiDQWmwhKkqsaf-Ww}{192.168.56.113}{192.168.56.113:9300}])

[2016-06-10 01:01:49,534][INFO ][cluster.service         ] [elasticsearch-node-
01] added {{elasticsearch-node-02}{XrtyRvgOS3yVX17AlNeOzQ}{192.168.56.112}{192.1
68.56.112:9300},}, reason: zen-disco-join(join from node[{elasticsearch-node-02}
{XrtyRvgOS3yVX17AlNeOzQ}{192.168.56.112}{192.168.56.112:9300}])
[2016-06-10 01:01:53,296][INFO ][cluster.routing.allocation] [elasticsearch-node
-01] Cluster health status changed from [RED] to [YELLOW] (reason: [shards start
ed [[twitter][2]] ...]).
█
```

"tailing" Elasticsearch log files

# grep

The `grep` command is a general purpose text search tool. One useful application of `grep` is to search through a directory of log files for a specific string. To *grep* or search `/var/log/elasticsearch` for all logged exceptions, run the following command with the `-r` (recursive) and `-i` (case insensitive search) options:

```
grep -ir exception /var/log/elasticsearch/*.log
```

Assuming there are some exceptions logged in your Elasticsearch log files, you should see something like this:

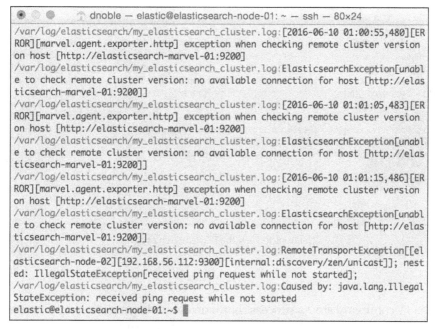

"grepping" log files for exceptions

# ps

Use the `ps` command along with the `grep` command to see whether a particular process is running. This is a useful sanity check if you are running into issues stopping or starting Elasticsearch (or another process).

To check whether Elasticsearch is running, use the following command:

```
ps -ef | grep -i elasticsearch
```

This command will output nothing if Elasticsearch is not running. If it's running, you should see something like this:

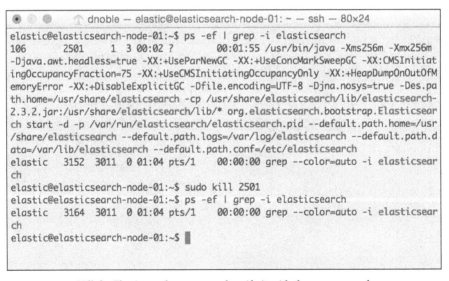

Using ps to view the Elasticsearch process

# kill

Use the `kill` command stop a process that won't shut down gracefully. For example, to shut down the Elasticsearch process listed previously, run the following command:

```
sudo kill 2501
```

Kill the Elasticsearch process and verify it with the ps command

# free

The `free` command tells us how much memory is in use on a system. Its usage is:

```
free -m
```

Running this command will yield something similar to:

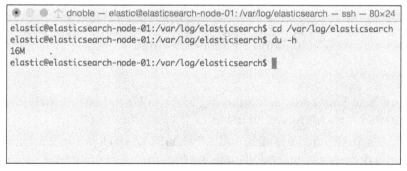

The free command shows the amount of RAM on the system

This output means that we are using 333 MB of our available 490 MB memory store.

# du and df

The `du` and `df` commands tell us how much disk space is available on the host. Use `du` to see how much data is stored in the current directory, as shown here:

```
cd /var/log/elasticsearch
du -h
```

You should see a result similar to this:

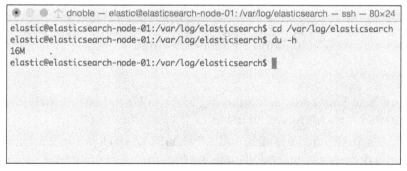

The du command calculates the size of a directory

In this case, there are 15 MB of log files in `/var/log/elasticsearch/`.

Use df to see how much disk space is available across the system, as shown here:

```
df -h
```

You should see a result similar to this:

```
dnoble — elastic@elasticsearch-node-01: /var/log/elasticsearch — ssh — 80×24
elastic@elasticsearch-node-01:/var/log/elasticsearch$ df -h
Filesystem                    Size  Used Avail Use% Mounted on
/dev/mapper/ubuntu--vg-root   7.0G  5.4G  1.3G  81% /
udev                          236M  4.0K  236M   1% /dev
tmpfs                          50M  320K   49M   1% /run
none                          5.0M     0  5.0M   0% /run/lock
none                          246M     0  246M   0% /run/shm
/dev/sda1                     228M   56M  161M  26% /boot
/dev/sdb1                     7.9G  2.0G  5.9G  25% /data2
elastic@elasticsearch-node-01:/var/log/elasticsearch$ ▊
```

Disk usage on elasticsearch-node-01

The output here says there is 1.3G of available storage left on the / mount point.

Note that in both of these commands, the -h flag stands for **human readable**, meaning they will output values in terms of KB, MB, or GB, as opposed to just bytes.

# Summary

This chapter examined the Elasticsearch monitoring tool Kopf, the Elasticsearch, Logstash, and Kibana (ELK) log aggregation stack, the system monitoring tool Nagios, and various GNU/Linux command line utilities.

Some takeaways are:

- Kopf is an Elasticsearch monitoring tool similar to Elasticsearch-head, but provides a few different metrics.

- The Elasticsearch, Logstash, and Kibana (ELK) stack is a tool for searching, analyzing, enriching, and visualizing log files.

- Consider using a tool such as Nagios to monitor an Elasticsearch cluster. Nagios can be configured to send out email notifications when a process goes down or if the node itself goes down.

- Using a few GNU/Linux command tools, we can gather many of the same metrics provided by the various Elasticsearch monitoring tools.

The next chapter will discuss troubleshooting Elasticsearch performance and reliability issues. The monitoring tools discussed in this chapter will be useful when tackling the real-world problems outlined in upcoming chapters.

# 6

# Troubleshooting Performance and Reliability Issues

This chapter focuses on troubleshooting common performance and reliability issues for Elasticsearch using case studies with real-world examples.

This chapter will help answer the following questions:

- How do I configure my Elasticsearch cluster to optimize performance?
- How do I prevent OutOfMemoryError exceptions?
- How does my data-indexing strategy affect cluster resources?
- Why are my queries running slow?
- How can I keep query performance strong when indexing a large amount of data?
- How can I configure indices to use less disk space?

## System configuration

Elasticsearch configuration may lead to a number of performance and reliability issues, as mentioned in *Chapter 2, Installation and the Requirements for Elasticsearch*. A quick reminder that the most important configuration changes to make to your cluster are as follows:

- Ensuring that the Elasticsearch heap size (ES_HEAP) is set to 1/2 of available system memory, but does not exceed 31 GB. Set this value in /etc/defaults/elasticsearch
- Disabling memory swapping
- Locking the Elasticsearch address space into memory by setting bootstrap.mlockall: true in elasticsearch.yml

Refer to *Chapter 2, Installation and the Requirements for Elasticsearch,* for more detailed instructions on how to set these values.

# The fielddata cache

A poorly configured Elasticsearch fielddata cache is often the reason for `OutOfMemoryError` exceptions.

When running a `sort` or `aggregation` (or `facet`) query, Elasticsearch fills the cache with all distinct field values from the query. This allows similar, subsequent queries to execute more quickly. However, Elasticsearch doesn't put an upper bound on the cache size by default; therefore, the data is not automatically evicted. If the cache causes the total JVM memory to fill up beyond the `ES_HEAP` size, the node will throw an `OutOfMemoryError` exception and will require an Elasticsearch restart.

To limit the fielddata cache size, set the `indices.fielddata.cache.size` value:

```
indices.fielddata.cache.size: 30%
```

This will limit the fielddata cache size to `30%` of the available JVM heap space.

You can set this value to a fixed value as well. For example, setting it to `10gb` will limit the cache size to no more than 10 gigabytes. The value that you choose will depend on the cluster and use case, but if you see an `OutOfMemoryError` caused by the fielddata cache overflowing, it's a good idea to set this field. The downside to limiting the fielddata cache is that it may affect query performance if a query needs to repopulate evicted fielddata cache items when the cache fills up.

If you see `OutOfMemoryError` logged to `/var/log/elasticsearch/`, you can check whether the fielddata cache is the problem by checking in Bigdesk or Marvel:

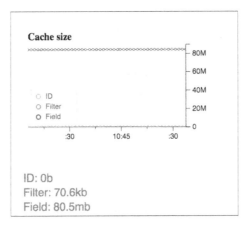

The fielddata cache in Bigdesk

The fielddata cache from the Marvel Kibana dashboard looks like this:

The fielddata cache in Marvel

 Do not change the `indices.fielddata.cache.expire` setting. This is a legacy setting to expire old cache values, and it does not provide any increase in performance. Elasticsearch developers stated that it will be deprecated in a future release.

You can also reduce the fielddata cache footprint by optimizing queries that use the cache.

For example, in our Twitter data, we have a `timestamp_ms` field, which stores the tweet's timestamp at millisecond precision. Because there are `86,400,000` milliseconds in a day, if we collected `5,000,000` Tweets in 24 hours, it's likely that the majority of these tweets will have a unique timestamp. If we run a query that sorts on this field, it will fill up the fielddata cache with as many as `5,000,000` distinct timestamps. This will quickly fill up the cache.

A more functional approach would be to store the timestamp field at either second or minute precision. Using second precision, the fielddata cache will be reduced from holding `5,000,000` unique timestamps to approximately `86,400` timestamps. Using minute precision will reduce it to only `1,440` unique timestamps.

Even after limiting the fielddata cache size to a fixed amount, you may still face `OutOfMemoryError` exceptions related to the field cache. This may be a result of a single query loading the fielddata cache with more data than it has been allocated.

This may happen if, for example, the fielddata cache is set to 2 GB, but we run a single query that tries to load 2.5 GB of data into the cache. This issue can be fixed by editing the fielddata circuit breaker in `elasticsearch.yml`.

The fielddata circuit breaker is set by default to 60% of the total JVM heap size:

```
indices.breaker.fielddata.limit: 60%
```

This way, if a single query's fielddata is more than 60% of the heap, the circuit breaker will trip and cause the query to throw an exception rather than causing an `OutOfMemoryError`. Using a lower percentage than the default 60% may help in solving `OutOfMemoryError` exceptions even when the fielddata cache is limited in size.

# Analyzing queries

Analyzing slow queries and improving their performance can be very challenging. This section examines how to look for the root cause of poor query performance, and it offers some different approaches to finding a solution.

# Slow log

If you notice poor query performance, start with the slow log. To enable the slow log, edit `elasticsearch.yml` and add these configuration options to all nodes on the cluster:

```
index.search.slowlog.threshold.query.warn: 8s
index.search.slowlog.threshold.query.info: 4s
index.search.slowlog.threshold.query.debug: 2s
index.search.slowlog.threshold.query.trace: 500ms

index.search.slowlog.threshold.fetch.warn: 1s
index.search.slowlog.threshold.fetch.info: 750ms
index.search.slowlog.threshold.fetch.debug: 500ms
index.search.slowlog.threshold.fetch.trace: 250ms

index.indexing.slowlog.threshold.index.warn: 8s
index.indexing.slowlog.threshold.index.info: 4s
index.indexing.slowlog.threshold.index.debug: 2s
index.indexing.slowlog.threshold.index.trace: 500ms
index.indexing.slowlog.level: info
index.indexing.slowlog.source: 5000
```

After updating `elasticsearch.yml` on all nodes, restart the cluster.

This configuration enables the slow log for three operations:

- **Query operations**: This is when Elasticsearch is performing the actual search for documents matching the query
- **Fetch operations**: This is when Elasticsearch fetches relevant documents from the index after finding documents of interest
- **Index operations**: This is when indexing new documents in Elasticsearch

We've also set a threshold level for each point: `warn`, `info`, `debug`, and `trace`. These levels identify the point at which Elasticsearch will write to the slow log. For example, if a query takes six seconds, based on our preceding configuration, the query will be logged at an `info` level. These levels make it possible to search for queries of a specific threshold.

Here's an example of searching the slow log for all queries that took longer than eight seconds, which were logged at the `warn` level:

```
grep "\[WARN \]"
    /var/log/elasticsearch/my_elasticsearch_cluster_*_slowlog.log*
```

Elasticsearch slow log for actions that took longer than eight seconds

The next section covers some additional approaches to improve query performance.

# Improving query performance

This section highlights common reasons behind certain slow queries on Elasticsearch, and offers instruction to improve performance.

## High-cardinality fields

As previously mentioned, running aggregation or sorts against high-cardinality fields (for example, dates precise to the millisecond) can fill up the fielddata cache which leads to `OutOfMemoryError` exceptions. However, even without these errors, running aggregations and sorts can be detrimental to performance. When it comes to dates, it's generally a good idea to store and use less precise dates in order to speed up query execution time.

## Querying smaller indices

As Elasticsearch indices grow larger, query performance will suffer. Another way to improve performance is to run queries against small indices. You can do this by storing our data in several smaller indices instead of one large one.

For example, with Twitter data, you can change the ingestion process to create a new index every day to store tweets. This way, we only query a subset of the total indices when running time-bounded queries.

Index templates are helpful in this case because they automatically apply a data mapping to new indices that follow a certain naming convention.

Let's create a new index template for our daily Twitter indices using the `twitter-YYmmdd` naming convention. Using this template, the `twitter-20160101` index will hold all tweets from January 1, 2016. Create this template with the following `curl` command:

```
curl -XPUT elasticsearch-node-01:9200/_template/template_1 -d '
{
    "template" : "twitter-*",
    "settings" : {
        "number_of_shards" : 5
    },
    "mappings" : {
        "twitter" : {
            "status" : {
                ...
```

```
            }

            . . .

        }

    }

}'
```

 Note the use of the * asterisk wildcard in the twitter-* template name. This wildcard that matches 0 or more characters, so it will match index names, such as twitter-20160101.

We can also create an index alias that allows us to query many or all of the indices at once.

The following example creates an alias using the * wildcard to query all available Twitter data:

```
curl -XPOST elasticsearch-node-01:9200/_aliases -d '{
    "actions" : [
        { "add" : { "index" : "twitter-*", "alias" : "all_twitter" } }
    ]
}'
```

Play around with different index sizes to find the best fit, depending on your data and setup. It's important to test how they affect your performance before committing to a particular index size because changing the indexing strategy later will involve re-indexing all of your data.

If you have a five-node cluster and collect 10,000 records per day, it makes sense to create new indices monthly versus daily to keep the number of indices down and to ensure that each individual index isn't too small. However, it's important to test all assumptions before committing to an indexing strategy. Use a tool such as Logstash and Kibana to monitor average query performance using different index sizes before making this decision.

# Cold indices

Sometimes, an Elasticsearch query is slow the first few times it runs, but it speeds up considerably afterwards. The lag occurs because the index is "cold" and the Elasticsearch caches are not populated with relevant data. After running the query a few times, Elasticsearch fills up the fielddata cache and other caches based on the query criteria. Subsequent queries with similar criteria will take advantage of these cached values and run faster as a result.

Elasticsearch "warmers" and "eager fielddata loading" solve the problem of cold indices by ensuring that the first time a user runs a query, required data for this query is already loaded in memory.

Indices can be cold for a variety of reasons:

- New data is indexed
- Automatic shard balancing and movement
- An Elasticsearch node restarted
- The cache was manually cleared

To demonstrate the performance gains of a slow aggregation query, use the following command:

```
curl -XPOST 'http://elasticsearch-node-01:9200/twitter/_cache/clear'


curl -XGET 'http://elasticsearch-node-01:9200/twitter/_search' -d '{
    "size" : 0,
    "query" : {
        "match_all" : {}
    },
    "aggs" : {
        "text" : {
            "terms" : {
                "field" : "text"
            }
        }
    }
}' | python -m json.tool
```

The results of this are as follows:

```
{
    ...
    "took": 5864
    ...
}
```

If we run the query a few more times, we'll start to see results like the following:

```
{
```

```
...
    "took": 529
...
}
```

This query took 5.8 seconds to finish at first, but after a few runs, it only took 0.529 seconds to complete. The initial slow query can be avoided and the performance can become more predictable after adding common queries to the Elasticsearch warmer. We'll demonstrate this by clearing the index cache again, then adding our query to the twitter index with the Elasticsearch Warmers API:

```
curl -XPOST 'http://elasticsearch-node-01:9200/twitter/_cache/clear'

curl -XPUT
  http://elasticsearch-node-01:9200/twitter/twitter/
  _warmer/text_agg_warmer?pretty -d '{
    "size" : 0,
    "query" : {
        "match_all" : {}
    },
    "aggs" : {
        "text" : {
            "terms" : {
                "field" : "text"
            }
        }
    }
}'
```

We can verify that the warmer query made it into our index by checking the Kopf **REGISTERED WARMERS** page at http://elasticsearch-node-01:9200/_ plugin/kopf and navigating to **more | warmers**.

This screenshot shows the warmer query on the Kopf warmers page:

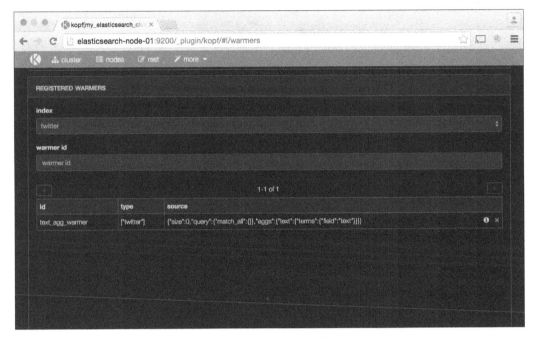

Viewing query warmers in Kopf

The warmer will take effect after restarting Elasticsearch. Run the query again to see a performance increase:

```
{
    ...
    "took": 418
    ...
}
```

This led to more than a 10x speedup, from 5.8 seconds to 0.41 seconds. We saw a similar increase after manually running the query a few times to populate the fielddata cache with data from the text field.

We can also enable eager fielddata loading for particular Elasticsearch fields:

```
curl -XPUT http://elasticsearch-node-01:9200/twitter/
  _mapping/twitter -d '{
    "text": {
        "type" : "string",
        "doc_values" : true,
```

```
    "fielddata" : {
        "loading" : "eager"
    }
  }
}'
```

If there are only a few distinct values for our fielddata cache, set the `loading` value to `eager_global_ordinals` for more memory optimization. After enabling either warming queries or eager fielddata loading, verify that the fielddata (and filter cache, in the case of warming queries) get populated by checking Marvel's node or Index statistics page or Bigdesk's fielddata chart.

> You can read more about warmers and eager field data loading at https://www.elastic.co/guide/en/elasticsearch/reference/current/indices-warmers.html and https://www.elastic.co/guide/en/elasticsearch/guide/current/preload-fielddata.html.

# The shard query cache

The shard query cache saves results for specific queries. Unlike the fielddata cache where any query that needs fielddata will speed up, with cached queries, we have to run the exact same query more than once to have a cache hit. Additionally, the entire query result is stored with the query cache. This is different from the fielddata cache, in which only part of the query result is stored. This means that the query cache will return results extremely quickly.

The shard query cache currently only stores hit counts, aggregations, and search suggestions. It does not store actual search results or hits. Moreover, the `search_type=count` query parameter is required when running cached queries. This may be updated in a future Elasticsearch release.

The query cache defaults to `1%` of the JVM heap, but it can be changed in `elasticsearch.yml`:

```
    indices.cache.query.size: 2%
```

The cache key is the JSON body of a search request. Even if a query is logically identical to a query already in the cache, if there is a difference in whitespace or key order, the cache will store these as two separate entries.

The shard query cache is disabled by default. To enable it on an existing index, run the following:

```
curl -XPUT elasticsearch-node-01:9200/twitter/_settings?pretty -d'{
    "index.cache.query.enable": true
}'
```

Or when creating a new index, add the same parameter to the settings section:

```
curl -XPUT elasticsearch-node-01:9200/twitter -d'
{
    ...
    "settings": {
        "index.cache.query.enable": true
    },
    ...
}'
```

When using the query cache, you will always receive the same up-to-date query results that you would get when running noncached queries. This is because cache entries are invalidated automatically when new data is loaded into a shard once the shard refreshes.

Run the text aggregation query again a few times, this time using the query cache:

```
curl -XGET
  'elasticsearch-node-01:9200/twitter/
  _search?search_type=count&query_cache=true' -d '{
    "size" : 2,
    "query" : {
        "match_all" : {}
    },
    "aggs" : {
        "text" : {
            "terms" : {
                "field" : "text"
            }
        }
    }
}' | python -m json.tool
```

After a few runs of this query, performance results like this should appear:

```
{
    ...
    "took": 4
    ...
}
```

The `4ms` response is an improvement from the `418ms` response using just the fielddata cache, and a huge improvement from the original `5.8` seconds against a cold Elasticsearch index.

>  Read more about the shard query cache at `https://www.elastic.co/guide/en/elasticsearch/reference/current/shard-request-cache.html`.

# Script queries

Script queries are a powerful way to query an index by running arbitrary code to manipulate or filter each hit the query comes across. However, they are also very costly, and they can hurt performance in large indices.

Whenever possible, it is best to avoid using scripts in Elasticsearch queries that need to return in a timely fashion. If you find yourself using them, try to think of ways to restructure your data to make them no longer necessary.

>  If you do use scripts in your application, make sure that you access source document fields with `doc["text"]` instead of `_source.text`; the latter will access the record on disk, while the former accesses it from memory.

# Testing meticulously

It's important to meticulously test each optimization strategy individually to see which is most effective. If you experience a slow query, try to recreate the problem on a smaller scale and test different optimizations until you find one that works. Make sure that you only test one change at a time in configuration or in query parameters. Also, run testing scripts for a long enough time period to account for normal deviation in performance due to garbage collection, cache evictions, and so on.

This approach to testing may feel tedious, but it will ultimately provide greater insight into the cluster, and it will help avoid making unnecessary changes to the system in the long run.

# System and data architecting

This section covers strategies to improve overall system performance, data indexing performance, and to maximize storage space.

## Hot-Warm architecture

For time-series data, including Twitter and other social media data as well as data from Logstash, Elastic.co recommends setting up what they have dubbed a **Hot-Warm** architecture. This setup puts nodes into three groups.

### Master nodes

Ideally, dedicate three nodes as master nodes that do not store data or fulfill queries. These machines don't need to be very powerful; they just perform cluster management operations.

### Hot nodes

Hot nodes hold the most recent data indices. All data writes are directed at these machines, and they are likely the most-frequently queried nodes. Elastic. co recommends equipping hot nodes with solid state drives (SSDs) for better I/O performance.

### Warm nodes

In this architecture, data is not being written to warm nodes; instead, they contain historical time-based data. For example, if we create a new Twitter index every day, we can move an index from "Hot" to "Warm" after seven days.

To configure a Hot node, add the following to `elasticsearch.yml`:

```
node.box_type: hot
```

Likewise, for a Warm node, add the following:

```
node.box_type: warm
```

To ensure that newly-created indices are allocated to the Hot nodes, configure the index on creation with the following:

```
curl -XPUT elasticsearch-node-01:9200/twitter-2016-03-06
{
    ...
    "settings": {
        "index.routing.allocation.require.box_type" : "hot"
    }
    ...
}
```

After seven days to move it to the Warm nodes, use the following:

```
curl -XPOST
  elasticsearch-node-01:9200/twitter-2016-03-06/_settings -d '{
    "settings": {
        "index.routing.allocation.require.box_type" : "warm"
    }
}'
```

Read more about the "Hot-Warm" architecture at `https://www.elastic.co/blog/hot-warm-architecture`.

# Reducing disk size

This section covers how to save disk space on your cluster.

## Compression

In Elasticsearch 2.0 and higher, you can increase the compression level for an index to reduce its footprint on disk. Unfortunately, this also makes indexing new data slower.

For use cases such as the preceding Hot-Warm architecture, it makes sense to increase the compression level on Warm nodes because they are less taxed than the Hot nodes.

To increase the compression level on an Elasticsearch 2.0+ node, perform the following:

1. Close the index.
2. Configure the `index.codec` setting to `best_compression`.
3. Re-open the index.

```
curl -XPOST elasticsearch-node-01:9200/twitter/_close
curl -XPUT elasticsearch-node-01:9200/twitter/_settings -d '{
    "settings": {
        "index.codec": "best_compression"
    }
}'
curl -XPOST elasticsearch-node-01:9200/twitter/_open
```

## Storing the _source and analyzed fields

By default, Elasticesarch stores all documents passed to it in the _source field and sets all fields to `analyzed`. This means that some basic tokenizers are run on the field. Disabling these options can save some disk space. We may decide to disable the _source field if we have documents stored elsewhere in our system. Or, we can disable the _source field and set the individual fields that we want to retrieve to `store: true`.

For the `analyzed` fields, think carefully about how you will use your data and set a field to `index: not_analyzed` if you don't need it tokenized. E-mail addresses, IP addresses, social media usernames, or other fields that we don't want to split up should be set to `not_analyzed`.

Create a new index with _source disabled, and set some fields to `not_analyzed`:

```
curl -XPOST elasticsearch-node-01:9200/newindex -d '{
    "mappings" : {
        "newtype" : {
            "_source" : {
                "enabled" : false
            },
            "properties" : {
                "username" : {
```

```
                "type" : "string",
                "index" : "not_analyzed",
                "store" : true
            },
            "text" : {
                "type" : "string"
            }
        }
      }
    }
}'
```

Unfortunately, there are some pretty big downsides to disabling the _source field. In addition to not being able to retrieve the full source during a query, the following are only supported if _source is enabled:

- The Elasticsearch update API
- Elasticsearch highlighting
- Many tools and strategies to re-index data

If disk space is a major concern, first check whether enabling data compression will meet your storage needs before disabling the _source field.

# Optimizing data ingestion

This section goes over some additional methods to improve data ingestion. In all of these methods, it's important to monitor the data ingestion rate to ensure that changes have the desired impact on performance.

As mentioned earlier, test one change at a time and run each test for a long enough period to return meaningful results. The best place to monitor ingestion performance is to select the index of interest in the Marvel *Indices* dashboard.

The following screenshot shows the Marvel Indices dashboard for our `twitter` data index:

Marvel indexing requests

Monitor this page in Marvel as you make changes to data ingest operations. This will allow you to see how changes affect the indexing rate in real time, and you'll be able to refer back to past indexing rate metrics for reference.

## Bulk indexing operations

For bulk indexing operations, test various ingestion sizes and monitor them in Marvel until you find the optimal size. For example, run tests at `1MB`, `5MB`, `10MB`, `15MB`, and `20MB` until you find the value that works best. If you run daily ingestion jobs, consider running them during off-peak hours so that resulting slowdowns affect fewer users.

After inserting data into Elasticsearch, the index must be refreshed before a user can see the data. By default, the refresh interval is set to once a second. This means that after indexing a document, it will appear in search results within one second.

Refreshing as often as once a second can hurt performance during large indexing operations. Lowering the refresh rate to a value such as `10s` or `30s` is worthwhile if your system doesn't need to display new results immediately after they are indexed.

Setting the refresh rate to `-1` will disable refreshing altogether. This can be useful for very large, one-time, or less-frequent periodic indexing operations. Remember to enable index refreshing afterwards.

To disable index refreshing, use the following:

```
curl -XPUT elasticsearch-node-01:9200/twitter/_settings -d '{
    "index" : {
        "refresh_interval" : "-1"
    }
}'
```

Turn enable index refreshing on afterwards:

```
curl -XPUT elasticsearch-node-01:9200/twitter/_settings -d '{
    "index" : {
        "refresh_interval" : "5s"
    }
}'
```

Warming queries are run every time an index is refreshed. Another option is to keep index refreshing on, disable warming queries during large index operations, and then re-enable warming when the indexing job is complete.

Disable index warmers:

```
curl -XPUT elasticsearch-node-01:9200/twitter/_settings -d '{
    "settings" : {
        "index.warmer.enabled" : "false"
    }
}'
```

Re-enable index warmers:

```
curl -XPUT elasticsearch-node-01:9200/twitter/_settings -d '{
    "settings" : {
        "index.warmer.enabled" : "true"
    }
}'
```

# Drive configuration

We mentioned in the "Hot-Warm" architecture section that SSDs are great for data indexing performance. Even if you don't use the "Hot-Warm" architecture, consider using SSDs for data nodes on your Elasticsearch cluster.

If SSDs are not an option, consider using fast hard drives (10,000+ RPM) configured in **RAID 0**. Remember that RAID 0 mirrors for performance, not reliability, but Elasticsearch's data replicas are sufficient for data reliability.

It's best to avoid storing data on network storage. If you run an Elasticsearch cluster on virtual machines, make sure that they use local disks for storage.

# Case studies

This section offers some real-world problem scenarios and solutions to use Elasticsearch.

# Node configuration

You have a five-node production cluster, where each node has 32GB of total memory and 16GB is allocated to Elasticsearch. Lately, you've noticed a problem: every couple of days, node-05 leaves the cluster without warning. Restarting Elasticsearch on this node solves the problem temporarily, but the node will drop out of the cluster again in a few days. How do we go about looking into this issue?

The next time this error happens, check the Elasticsearch logs before restarting the node:

```
tail -n 500  /var/log/elasticsearch/*.log
```

You notice in the log file that Elasticsearch is throwing an OutOfMemoryError exception, like the following:

```
Caused by: java.lang.OutOfMemoryError: Java heap space
        at org.apache.lucene.store.DataOutput.copyBytes
          (DataOutput.java:273)
        at org.apache.lucene.util.fst.FST.<init>(FST.java:342)
        at org.apache.lucene.util.fst.FST.<init>(FST.java:321)
```

You know that running out of fielddata can cause OutOfMemoryError exceptions, so after checking the elasticsearch.yml file, you find the following:

```
# indices.fielddata.cache.size: 30%
```

The cache setting was commented out. Uncomment this line and restart the Elasticsearch node. This seems to solve the problem at first. However, after two weeks, another `OutOfMemoryError` from `node-05` appears. After restarting the node, log into Bigdesk for insight. Clicking on `node-05`, you see the following:

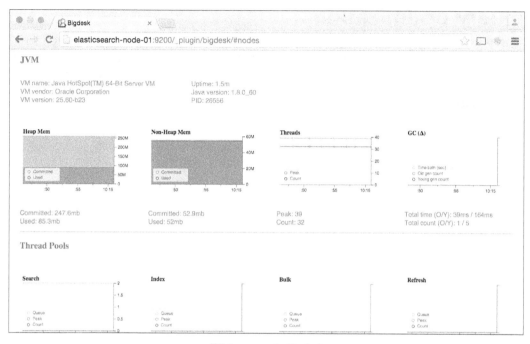

JVM memory in Bigdesk

It doesn't look like Elasticsearch is using much of the available memory, but this is probably because the node was just restarted.

Note that the maximum heap memory available for `node-05` is only about `250MB`. This is odd, considering the host has `32GB` of system memory. At this point, you want to ensure that the `ES_HEAP` variable was set properly. Open the following file:

```
/etc/default/elasticsearch
```

You will see the following:

```
# ES_HEAP_SIZE=16g
```

It looks like this configuration, like the `indices.fielddata.cache.size`, was also commented out. Uncommenting this line and restarting Elasticsearch brings the node's total available memory to `16GB`, and eliminates the `OutOfMemoryError` exceptions.

As mentioned earlier, node configuration errors are one of the most common reasons for poor Elasticsearch performance or crashes. It's important to validate each configuration change after it is made.

# Query optimization

You found a problem in one of your company's internal enterprise Elasticsearch web applications. First thing in the morning, the web application takes a long time to load query results. Performance starts to improve only after running a few queries.

To tackle this problem, take a look at the slow log. In one of the nodes, you see a query that takes 4.7 seconds to run as an INFO event in the log:

```
[2016-02-29 16:52:43,569][INFO ][index.search.slowlog.query]
  [elasticsearch-node-03] [twitter][1] took[4.7s],
  took_millis[4709], types[], stats[],
  search_type[QUERY_THEN_FETCH], total_shards[3],
  source[{"size":0,"query":{"match_all":{}},"aggs":{"screen_name":
  {"terms":{"field":"user.screen_name"}},"text":
  {"terms":{"field":"text"}}}}], extra_source[],
```

 The slow log won't necessarily write entries to all nodes, so check the log on each host.

Use `python -m json.tool` to pretty-print the query:

```
echo '{"size":0,"query":{"match_all":{}},"aggs":{"screen_name":{
  "terms":{"field":"user.screen_name"}},"text":{
  "terms":{"field":"text"}}}}' | python -m json.tool
```

You will see the following:

```
{
    "aggs": {
        "screen_name": {
            "terms": {
                "field": "user.screen_name"
            }
        },
        "text": {
            "terms": {
                "field": "text"
            }
        }
```

```
    },
    "query": {
        "match_all": {}
    },
    "size": 0
}
```

This `aggs` parameters may mean that this query makes heavy use of the field data cache. Diagnose this query and figure out what is causing the performance issue.

First, clear the fielddata cache to ensure consistent results:

```
curl -XPOST 'http://elasticsearch-node-01:9200/twitter/_cache/clear'
```

Now, run the query, as follows:

```
curl -XGET 'http://elasticsearch-node-01:9200/twitter/_search' -d '{
    "size" : 0,
    "query" : {
        "match_all" : {}
    },
    "aggs" : {
        "screen_name" : {
            "terms" : {
                "field" : "user.screen_name"
            }
        },
        "text" : {
            "terms" : {
                "field" : "text"
            }
        }
    }
}' | python -m json.tool
```

Results will be as follows:

```
{
    ...
    "took": 4183
    ...
}
```

After running the query a few more times to ensure that the values it needs are in the fielddata cache, the query runs in around .6 seconds. This is a pretty good improvement. Verify that the fielddata cache is now populated using Bigdesk or Marvel (refer to images for fielddata cache for Bigdesk and Marvel).

The fielddata cache was probably getting cleared due to new data ingestion or shard relocation overnight. To solve this problem, enable eager fielddata loading on both the `user.screen_name` and `text` fields in the Elasticsearch mapping.

However, this query's performance still isn't great. Checking the slow log again, we note it still triggers a TRACE event:

```
[2016-02-29 16:54:20,069] [TRACE] [index.search.slowlog.query]
  [elasticsearch-node-03] [twitter] [1] took[680ms],
  took_millis[680], types[], stats[],
  search_type[QUERY_THEN_FETCH], total_shards[3],
  source[{"size":0,"query":{"match_all":{}},"aggs":
  {"screen_name":{"terms":{"field":"user.screen_name"}},"text":
  {"terms":{"field":"text"}}}}], extra_source[],
```

To figure out why this query takes over 0.5 seconds to run even after the fielddata cache is populated, break the query down into individual queries — one that runs the `text` aggregation, and another that runs the `screen_name` aggregation:

```
curl -XGET 'http://elasticsearch-node-01:9200/twitter/_search' -d '{
    "size" : 0,
    "query" : {
        "match_all" : {}
    },
    "aggs" : {
        "text" : {
            "terms" : {
                "field" : "text"
            }
        }
    }
}' | python -m json.tool
```

This query takes approximately .4 seconds to run:

```
curl -XGET 'http://elasticsearch-node-01:9200/twitter/_search' -d '{
    "size" : 0,
    "query" : {
```

```
        "match_all" : {}
    },
    "aggs" : {
        "screen_name" : {
            "terms" : {
                "field" : "user.screen_name"
            }
        }
    }
}
}' | python -m json.tool
```

This query runs in `.08` seconds; this is a vast improvement over the `text` aggregation query.

As we've identified the `text` aggregation as the slow part of the query, consider removing that operation and finding another solution which will yield similar results. Although it depends what the aggregation is used for, aggregating on a lower-cardinality field may be a suitable solution. For example, if the `text` aggregation is used to build a word cloud, consider instead using the `entities.hashtags.text` hashtag field to get a similar result.

Another option is keeping the `text` aggregation, but running it periodically in the background and caching the results.

Finally, consider using the shard query cache on this query. As no queries are returned (`size=0`), we can enable the `search_type=count` and `query_cache=true` parameter to cache the results of the aggregation.

# Web application performance

You are working on a web application that searches Twitter data in an Elasticsearch index. In addition to displaying tweets in the search results page, you want to display:

- Tweet activity over time
- Top users in the results
- Top hashtags in the results
- Top user mentions

We can implement all of these items using Elasticsearch aggregations, but these operations are much more costly than simply running a search for hits.

To speed up page load times, we split this into two AJAX requests: one query for results, and one query for all aggregations. The queries are both AJAX requests, meaning that the page will load immediately. The query results will follow shortly after, and the aggregation results will load last. Because the aggregations query doesn't return any hits, we can set the parameters `search_type=count` and `query_cache=true` to cache the aggregations for future queries.

When paging through results, make sure to only query for the hits and not for the aggregation results. Aggregation results will stay the same no matter what page of data is being looked at.

# Summary

This chapter addressed some common performance and reliability issues that come up when using Elasticsearch. To reiterate some of the major points in this chapter:

- Always double-check your Elasticsearch cluster's configuration for errors

- Set the fielddata cache size, especially if you see `OutOfMemoryError` exceptions

- Use the slow log to find what queries run slow on your cluster

- Avoid aggregations on high-cardinality fields (such as millisecond timestamps)

- Be cognizant of your data indexing strategy so that no one index grows too large

- Use index warmers or enable `eager_global_ordinals` to ensure queries that use the fielddata cache are fast the first time we run them

- If possible, use SSDs on nodes that index data, and avoid storing Elasticsearch indices on network storage

Most importantly, when diagnosing Elasticsearch issues, be meticulous about testing at each stage. For example, don't try to optimize a query by making changes to `elasticsearch.yml`, modifying the query criteria, and enabling index `warmers` all at once before running the query again. Test one variable at a time to extract precisely where the problem is before deciding how to fix it.

The next chapter discusses how to understand and fix node failures after they've already happened.

# 7
# Node Failure and Post-Mortem Analysis

In the previous chapter, we learned how to troubleshoot common performance and reliability issues that come up when using Elasticsearch using case studies with real-world examples. This chapter explores some common causes of node and cluster failures. Specific topics covered are as follows:

- How to determine the root cause of a failure
- How to take corrective action for node failures
- Case studies with real-world examples of diagnosing system failures

## Diagnosing problems

Elasticsearch node failures can manifest in many different ways. Some of the symptoms of node failures are as follows:

- A node crashes during heavy data indexing
- Elasticsearch process stops running for an unknown reason
- A cluster won't recover from a yellow or red state
- Query requests time out
- Index requests time out

When a node in your cluster experiences problems such as these, it can be tempting to just restart Elasticsearch or the node itself and move on like nothing happened. However, without addressing the underlying issue, the problem is likely to resurface in the future. If you encounter scenarios such as the ones just listed, check the health of your cluster in the following manner:

- Check the cluster health with Elasticsearch-head or Kopf
- Check the historical health with Marvel
- Check for Nagios alerts
- Check Elasticsearch log files
- Check system log files
- Check the system health using command-line tools

These steps will help diagnose the root cause of problems in your cluster. In this section, we'll look at some underlying causes that lead to node failure, including the following:

- Out-of-memory errors
- Not enough system memory available
- Resource contention
- Running out of disk space

# OutOfMemoryError exceptions

If a node throws an `OutOfMemoryError`, the immediate fix is to restart it. However, it's not always obvious when or why a node encounters this error. Symptoms include the following:

- Shard failures
- Search query failures
- Indexing failures

Often, there will be no immediate symptoms at all. Unfortunately, checking Elasticsearch-head, Marvel, and Bigdesk won't tell you outright that an `OutOfMemoryError` exception has occurred, but they can give us some warning signs that one *may* have occurred. To be sure that an `OutOfMemoryError` exception has occurred, check the Elasticsearch logs.

# Shard failures

One sign that an `OutOfMemoryError` exception has occurred is the appearance of shard failures in query responses. This response indicates shard failures in the `_shards.failed` key, and it describes the failure in `_shards.failures`.

The following example query shows what a shard failure looks like in a query response:

```
curl -XGET http://elasticsearch-node-01:9200/twitter/_search?size=0
{
    "_shards": {
        "failed": 1,
        "failures": [
            {
                "index": "twitter",
                "reason": "NodeDisconnectedException[[elasticsearch-
node-03][inet[elasticsearch-node-03/192.168.56.113:9300]][indices:data/
read/search[phase/query]] disconnected]",
                "shard": 1,
                "status": 500
            }
        ],
        "successful": 2,
        "total": 3
    },
    "hits": {
        ...
        "total": 10803
    },
    ...
}
```

Note that even though a shard failed in this query, it still returned results. However, because there are three total shards and only two returned data successfully, the query results are not representative of all data in the index.

Sometimes, if the cluster is in a red state, for example, the `_shards` object will indicate fewer successful shards than the total available shards but won't report an error. Take a look a the following code where `_shards.successful` is less than `_shards.total`, but `_shards.failed` is set to `0`:

```
{
    "_shards": {
        "failed": 0,
        "successful": 2,
        "total": 3
    },
    "hits": {
        ...
        "total": 10803
    },
    ...
}
```

In both of these cases, the `hits.total` value is only representative of approximately two thirds of our actual total data count.

When we encounter shard failures or shards that don't return data successfully, it's a good idea to use Elasticsearch-head to check the state of our cluster. Elasticsearch-head may look something like the following:

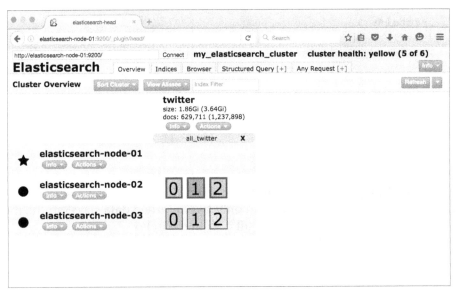

Shards relocating in Elasticsearch-head

In this screenshot, we can see that all shards are now available, but the cluster is still recovering and there aren't any shards assigned to `elasticsearch-node-01`. At this point, we may also notice that the cluster takes a very long time to return to a green state, or possibly never returns to a green state. This problem may be due to a node that is out of heap space failing to relocate one of its shards to another node with more memory.

Next, open Elasticsearch-kopf to get a more detailed view of our nodes:

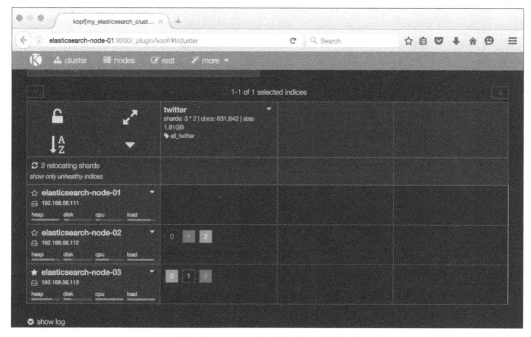

Shards relocating in Elasticsearch-kopf

In Elasticsearch-kopf, we see high heap usage on `elasticsearch-node-01` and `elasticsearch-node-02`, which is a good indicator that an `OutOfMemoryError` exception has occurred. Checking the logs, we confirm that an `OutOfMemoryError` was thrown on `elasticsearch-node-01`:

```
marking and sending shard failed due to [engine failure, reason [already closed by tragic event on
the index writer]]
java.lang.OutOfMemoryError: Java heap space
[2016-04-28 21:51:14,801][WARN ][cluster.action.shard    ] [elasticsearch-node-01] [twitter][0] re
ceived shard failed for target shard [[twitter][0], node[coGMtjheS6ZRzOOQBjtDEg], [R], v[258], s[ST
ARTED], a[id=dMXtLk25QoSPf5Vw3aRiDQ]], indexUUID [mfsJtjfDRtCbOWTgFuFhpQ], message [failed to perfo
rm indices:data/write/bulk[s] on replica on node {elasticsearch-node-01}{coGMtjheS6ZRzOOQBjtDEg}{19
2.168.56.111}{192.168.56.111:9300}], failure [RemoteTransportException[[elasticsearch-node-01][192.
168.56.111:9300][indices:data/write/bulk[s][r]]]; nested: IndexFailedEngineException[Index failed f
or [status#725864975173033984]]; nested: OutOfMemoryError[Java heap space]; ]
RemoteTransportException[[elasticsearch-node-01][192.168.56.111:9300][indices:data/write/bulk[s][r]
]]; nested: IndexFailedEngineException[Index failed for [status#725864975173033984]]; nested: OutOf
MemoryError[Java heap space];
Caused by: [twitter][[twitter][0]] IndexFailedEngineException[Index failed for [status#725864975173
033984]]; nested: OutOfMemoryError[Java heap space];
        at org.elasticsearch.index.engine.InternalEngine.index(InternalEngine.java:462)
        at org.elasticsearch.index.shard.IndexShard.index(IndexShard.java:601)
        at org.elasticsearch.index.engine.Engine$Index.execute(Engine.java:836)
        at org.elasticsearch.action.index.TransportIndexAction.executeIndexRequestOnReplica(Transpo
rtIndexAction.java:196)
        at org.elasticsearch.action.bulk.TransportShardBulkAction.shardOperationOnReplica(Transport
ShardBulkAction.java:436)
        at org.elasticsearch.action.bulk.TransportShardBulkAction.shardOperationOnReplica(Transport
ShardBulkAction.java:68)
:
```

Examining the Elasticsearch logs shows an OutOfMemoryError

Additionally, we see several other Exceptions recorded in the log file that start appearing after the `OutOfMemoryError`, like in the following screenshot:

```
nection
java.lang.IllegalStateException: Message not fully read (request) for requestId [46637], action [in
ternal:index/shard/recovery/file_chunk], readerIndex [4119] vs expected [398521]; resetting
        at org.elasticsearch.transport.netty.MessageChannelHandler.messageReceived(MessageChannelHa
ndler.java:121)
        at org.jboss.netty.channel.SimpleChannelUpstreamHandler.handleUpstream(SimpleChannelUpstrea
mHandler.java:70)
        at org.jboss.netty.channel.DefaultChannelPipeline.sendUpstream(DefaultChannelPipeline.java:
564)
        at org.jboss.netty.channel.DefaultChannelPipeline$DefaultChannelHandlerContext.sendUpstream
(DefaultChannelPipeline.java:791)
        at org.jboss.netty.channel.Channels.fireMessageReceived(Channels.java:296)
        at org.jboss.netty.handler.codec.frame.FrameDecoder.unfoldAndFireMessageReceived(FrameDecod
er.java:462)
        at org.jboss.netty.handler.codec.frame.FrameDecoder.callDecode(FrameDecoder.java:443)
        at org.jboss.netty.handler.codec.frame.FrameDecoder.messageReceived(FrameDecoder.java:310)
        at org.jboss.netty.channel.SimpleChannelUpstreamHandler.handleUpstream(SimpleChannelUpstrea
mHandler.java:70)
        at org.jboss.netty.channel.DefaultChannelPipeline.sendUpstream(DefaultChannelPipeline.java:
564)
        at org.jboss.netty.channel.DefaultChannelPipeline$DefaultChannelHandlerContext.sendUpstream
(DefaultChannelPipeline.java:791)
        at org.elasticsearch.common.netty.OpenChannelsHandler.handleUpstream(OpenChannelsHandler.ja
va:75)
:
```

Additional errors in the Elasticsearch log related to OutOfMemoryError

Continuing to examine the log file, we see an error indicating shard failure due to the node running out of memory:

Shard failure errors in the Elasticsearch log

# Slow queries

Slow queries are another sign that an `OutOfMemoryError` has occurred. In the previous example, checking the slow-log file with the Unix `less` command on `elasticsearch-node-02` shows the following:

```
less my_elasticsearch_cluster_index_search_slowlog.log.2016-04-28
```

Slow queries may indicate that an error has occurred

Checking the Elasticsearch log on `elasticsearch-node-02`, we can verify that an `OutOfMemoryError` was captured:

```
● ● ●                    dnoble — elastic@elasticsearch-node-02: ~ — ssh — 99×25
RemoteTransportException[[elasticsearch-node-01][192.168.56.111:9300][indices:data/write/bulk[s][r]
]]; nested: IndexFailedEngineException[Index failed for [status#725865298138550272]]; nested: OutOf
MemoryError[Java heap space];
Caused by: [twitter][[twitter][2]] IndexFailedEngineException[Index failed for [status#725865298138
550272]]; nested: OutOfMemoryError[Java heap space];
        at org.elasticsearch.index.engine.InternalEngine.index(InternalEngine.java:462)
        at org.elasticsearch.index.shard.IndexShard.index(IndexShard.java:601)
        at org.elasticsearch.index.engine.Engine$Index.execute(Engine.java:836)
        at org.elasticsearch.action.index.TransportIndexAction.executeIndexRequestOnReplica(Transpo
rtIndexAction.java:196)
        at org.elasticsearch.action.bulk.TransportShardBulkAction.shardOperationOnReplica(Transport
ShardBulkAction.java:436)
        at org.elasticsearch.action.bulk.TransportShardBulkAction.shardOperationOnReplica(Transport
ShardBulkAction.java:68)
        at org.elasticsearch.action.support.replication.TransportReplicationAction$AsyncReplicaActi
on.doRun(TransportReplicationAction.java:392)
        at org.elasticsearch.common.util.concurrent.AbstractRunnable.run(AbstractRunnable.java:37)
        at org.elasticsearch.action.support.replication.TransportReplicationAction$ReplicaOperation
TransportHandler.messageReceived(TransportReplicationAction.java:291)
        at org.elasticsearch.action.support.replication.TransportReplicationAction$ReplicaOperation
TransportHandler.messageReceived(TransportReplicationAction.java:283)
        at org.elasticsearch.transport.RequestHandlerRegistry.processMessageReceived(RequestHandler
Registry.java:75)
        at org.elasticsearch.transport.netty.MessageChannelHandler$RequestHandler.doRun(MessageChan
:█
```

Verifying that Elasticsearch threw an exception

# Resolving OutOfMemoryError exceptions

As mentioned earlier, when you see an `OutOfMemoryError`, it's best to restart the node to prevent further exceptions. However, this is only a temporary fix. It's important to also fix the underlying issue that is causing the error. Refer to *Chapter 6, Troubleshooting Performance and Reliability Issues*, for more strategies about solving `OutOfMemoryError` exceptions. A few strategies are listed, as follows:

- Limit the size of the field data cache
- Enable circuit breakers for the field data cache
- Adjust the size and frequency of bulk data inserts
- Reduce the number of total shards
- Ensure that `ES_HEAP_SIZE` is properly set
- Ensure that there is enough physical memory available to the machine

After seeing errors in the log, we can correlate their timestamps with Marvel to see what kind of activity was going on when the error occurred. For example, let's suppose that we see the following `OutOfMemoryError`:

```
● ◉ ◎        ⋔ dnoble — elastic@elasticsearch-node-01: /home/humangeo — ssh — 99×25
[2016-04-29 15:26:39,788][WARN ][indices.cluster        ] [elasticsearch-node-01] [[twitter2][0]] ▦
 marking and sending shard failed due to [engine failure, reason [out of memory (source: [index])]]
java.lang.OutOfMemoryError: Java heap space
        at org.apache.lucene.index.FreqProxTermsWriterPerField$FreqProxPostingsArray.<init>(FreqPro
xTermsWriterPerField.java:212)
        at org.apache.lucene.index.FreqProxTermsWriterPerField$FreqProxPostingsArray.newInstance(Fr
eqProxTermsWriterPerField.java:232)
        at org.apache.lucene.index.ParallelPostingsArray.grow(ParallelPostingsArray.java:48)
        at org.apache.lucene.index.TermsHashPerField$PostingsBytesStartArray.grow(TermsHashPerField
.java:251)
        at org.apache.lucene.util.BytesRefHash.add(BytesRefHash.java:292)
        at org.apache.lucene.index.TermsHashPerField.add(TermsHashPerField.java:150)
        at org.apache.lucene.index.DefaultIndexingChain$PerField.invert(DefaultIndexingChain.java:6
82)
        at org.apache.lucene.index.DefaultIndexingChain.processField(DefaultIndexingChain.java:365)
        at org.apache.lucene.index.DefaultIndexingChain.processDocument(DefaultIndexingChain.java:3
21)
        at org.apache.lucene.index.DocumentsWriterPerThread.updateDocument(DocumentsWriterPerThread
.java:234)
        at org.apache.lucene.index.DocumentsWriter.updateDocument(DocumentsWriter.java:450)
        at org.apache.lucene.index.IndexWriter.updateDocument(IndexWriter.java:1477)
        at org.apache.lucene.index.IndexWriter.addDocument(IndexWriter.java:1256)
        at org.elasticsearch.index.engine.InternalEngine.innerIndex(InternalEngine.java:530)
        at org.elasticsearch.index.engine.InternalEngine.index(InternalEngine.java:454)
:▊
```

An OutOfMemoryError exception occurred at 4/29/2016 15:26:39

We can check Marvel's activity around the `4/29/2016 15:26:39` timeframe. In this case, we'll set it from `2016-04-29 15:25:00` to `2016-04-29 15:27:30`, as shown in the following screenshot:

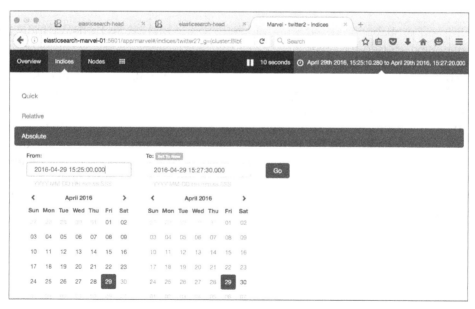

Change the date range in Marvel

Although we see no search activities taking place in the index at the time of the collapse, a modest **Indexing Rate** is followed by a drop-off in indexing activity:

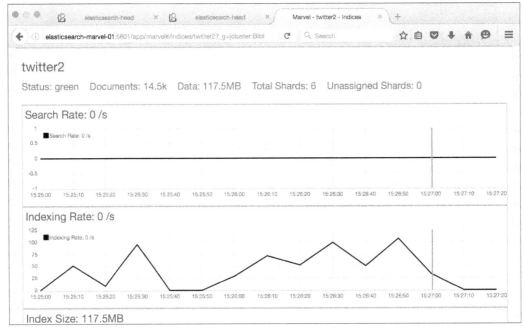

Investigating with Marvel

The drop-off probably occurred after the OutOfMemoryError, and a heavy indexing load may have caused the error.

As OutOfMemoryError exceptions may not occur very frequently, it can be difficult to know for sure whether applying the fixes that we implemented successfully resolved the issue. To ensure that the issue is completely solved, it's best to find a way to reliably recreate the error. Then, adjust Elasticsearch configuration settings and load until you don't see the issue any more. It's often possible to recreate the issue by standing up a simple single-node cluster with a similar configuration and load as a node in the primary cluster. In the previous example, we might try to verify that data bulk loading caused the exception by indexing documents at a similar rate into a single-node test cluster in a controlled environment.

# Elasticsearch process crashes

If the Elasticsearch process unexpectedly stops running, it may be because the operating system killed it. In these cases, the Elasticsearch log file may not have any useful information about the error, and we instead have to check the `syslog`:

```
sudo tail -n200 /var/log/syslog
```

```
View the last 200 lines of /var/log/syslog
```

```
...
```

```
Apr 29 14:56:00 elasticsearch-node-01 kernel: [39935.321257]
  Out of memory: Kill process 5969 (java) score 446 or
  sacrifice child
```

```
Apr 29 14:56:00 elasticsearch-node-01 kernel:
  [39935.321343] Killed process 5969 (java) total-vm:2361960kB,
  anon-rss:441676kB, file-rss:14392kB
```

This can happen if Elasticsearch tries to claim more system memory than the memory available, and this is often a result of an improperly set `ES_HEAP_SIZE` or resource contention with other processes. If your cluster experiences this issue and there are other memory-heavy processes running on the cluster, it may be a good idea to move these processes off the Elasticsearch cluster. To verify that Elasticsearch was forcibly stopped by the operating system, check the `syslog` file at `/var/log/syslog`:

```
dnoble — elastic@elasticsearch-node-01: /home/humangeo — ssh — 99×25
Apr 29 14:55:34 elasticsearch-node-01 kernel: [39909.742047] Out of memory: Kill process 5878 (java
) score 446 or sacrifice child
Apr 29 14:55:34 elasticsearch-node-01 kernel: [39909.742175] Killed process 5878 (java) total-vm:24
66124kB, anon-rss:441568kB, file-rss:14336kB
Apr 29 14:56:00 elasticsearch-node-01 kernel: [39935.320173] java invoked oom-killer: gfp_mask=0x28
0da, order=0, oom_score_adj=0
Apr 29 14:56:00 elasticsearch-node-01 kernel: [39935.320179] java cpuset=/ mems_allowed=0
Apr 29 14:56:00 elasticsearch-node-01 kernel: [39935.320183] Pid: 5971, comm: java Not tainted 3.8.
0-44-generic #66~precise1-Ubuntu
Apr 29 14:56:00 elasticsearch-node-01 kernel: [39935.320186] Call Trace:
Apr 29 14:56:00 elasticsearch-node-01 kernel: [39935.320196]  [<ffffffff816e2ad8>] dump_header+0x83
/0xbb
Apr 29 14:56:00 elasticsearch-node-01 kernel: [39935.320201]  [<ffffffff816e2b65>] oom_kill_process
.part.6+0x55/0x2cf
Apr 29 14:56:00 elasticsearch-node-01 kernel: [39935.320208]  [<ffffffff8113940d>] oom_kill_process
+0x4d/0x50
Apr 29 14:56:00 elasticsearch-node-01 kernel: [39935.320213]  [<ffffffff81139745>] out_of_memory+0x
145/0x1d0
Apr 29 14:56:00 elasticsearch-node-01 kernel: [39935.320219]  [<ffffffff8113efa7>] __alloc_pages_no
demask+0x977/0x990
Apr 29 14:56:00 elasticsearch-node-01 kernel: [39935.320226]  [<ffffffff8117dc33>] alloc_pages_vma+
0xa3/0x150
Apr 29 14:56:00 elasticsearch-node-01 kernel: [39935.320232]  [<ffffffff8115becb>] do_anonymous_pag
e.isra.37+0x7b/0x2f0
:
```

Operating-system killed Elasticsearch process due to running out of memory

Take the following line:

```
Apr 29 14:55:34 elasticsearch-node-01 kernel: [39909.742047]
  Out of memory: Kill process 5878 (java) score 446 or
  sacrifice child
```

This line indicates that the operating system killed the Elasticsearch process. In this case, we won't see any corresponding log entries in the Elasticsearch log files.

# Disk space

When a node runs out of disk space, it will stay in the cluster and can still handle index and search requests, but it offloads its shards to other nodes in the cluster. As the cluster reallocates shards, queries may run slow or timeout. Once shards are reallocated to other nodes in the cluster, you'll likely see some performance degradation as the cluster is operating with one less data node.

A node running out of disk space can be dangerous if all nodes are configured with the same amount of space. If one node runs out of space, it's likely that other nodes in the cluster are running low on disk space too. Once the cluster finishes reallocating shards to other nodes in the cluster, it can cause these nodes to run out of space as well. This causes a chain reaction that ultimately results in the entire cluster going down.

We can check whether a node is running low on disk space using Kopf or Marvel or by configuring a Nagios alert. Additionally, we'll see an error in the Elasticsearch log related to low disk space, as seen in the following screenshot:

Kopf shows that `elasticsearch-node-01` is low on disk space

# Resolving the issue

Disk space issues can be grouped into two categories:

1. Elasticsearch has too much data loaded into it and is filling up the disk.

2. Something other than Elasticsearch data is filling up the disk, for example, a large log file.

To resolve the first category issues, one solution is to increase the node's storage capacity by adding another drive or volume to the node and configuring Elasticsearch to use the space. For example, if we mount additional storage at /data, update the elasticsearch.yml configuration file to use it as follows:

```
path.data: /var/lib/elasticsearch,/data
```

Restart Elasticsearch on the node. The node will then distribute its data across the two data directories.

For the second category, if the cause is external to Elasticsearch, removing the offending files to clear up disk space will be enough to get Elasticsearch going again. There's no need to restart the node.

Some additional measures we can take to reduce disk space usage are as follows:

- Add additional nodes to the cluster.

- Decrease shard replication; for example, from two replicas to one replica.

- Ensure that individual shards don't grow too big by breaking large indices into smaller indices. For example, instead of storing all Twitter data in one index, create a new index every month to store new data.

- Enable data compression (refer to *Chapter 6, Troubleshooting Performance and Reliability Issues*).

# Reviewing some case studies

This section discusses some real-world scenarios of Elasticsearch node failure and how to address them.

# The ES process quits unexpectedly

A few weeks ago we noticed in Marvel that the Elasticsearch process was down on one of our nodes. We restarted Elasticsearch on this node, and everything seemed to return to normal. However, checking Marvel later on in the week, we notice that the node is down again. We decide to look at the Elasticsearch log files, but don't notice any exceptions. As we don't see anything in the Elasticsearch log, we suspect that the operating system may have killed Elasticsearch. Checking `syslog` at `/var/log/syslog`, we see the error:

```
Out of memory: Kill process 5969 (java) score 446 or sacrifice child
```

This verifies that the operating system killed Elasticsearch because the system was running out of memory. We check the Elasticsearch configuration and don't see any issues. This node is configured in the same way as the other nodes in the cluster. Next, we check for resource contention with other processes by running the `top` command and get the following results:

```
● ● ●        ⬆ dnoble — elastic@elasticsearch-node-01: ~ — ssh — 80×23
Tasks:  92 total,   4 running,  88 sleeping,   0 stopped,   0 zombie
Cpu(s):  4.4%us,  0.4%sy,  0.0%ni, 94.9%id,  0.1%wa,  0.0%hi,  0.2%si,  0.0%st
Mem:    502636k total,   496432k used,     6204k free,      68k buffers
Swap:   520188k total,    95644k used,   424544k free,    8416k cached

  PID USER      PR  NI  VIRT  RES  SHR S %CPU %MEM    TIME+  COMMAND
 8083 mysqldb   20   0  333m 326m   12 R 47.6 66.5  9:17.46 mysqld
 8120 elastics  20   0 2182m 104m 3608 S 45.7 21.2  0:08.08 java
   25 root      20   0     0    0    0 R  3.8  0.0  0:13.99 kswapd0
 8145 elastic   20   0 17332 1244  944 R  1.9  0.2  0:00.02 top
    1 root      20   0 24332   32   32 S  0.0  0.0  0:00.63 init
    2 root      20   0     0    0    0 S  0.0  0.0  0:00.00 kthreadd
    3 root      20   0     0    0    0 S  0.0  0.0  0:15.00 ksoftirqd/0
    5 root       0 -20     0    0    0 S  0.0  0.0  0:00.00 kworker/0:0H
    7 root       0 -20     0    0    0 S  0.0  0.0  0:00.00 kworker/u:0H
    8 root      RT   0     0    0    0 S  0.0  0.0  0:00.00 migration/0
    9 root      20   0     0    0    0 S  0.0  0.0  0:00.00 rcu_bh
   10 root      20   0     0    0    0 R  0.0  0.0  0:22.82 rcu_sched
   11 root      RT   0     0    0    0 S  0.0  0.0  0:05.28 watchdog/0
   12 root       0 -20     0    0    0 S  0.0  0.0  0:00.00 cpuset
   13 root       0 -20     0    0    0 S  0.0  0.0  0:00.00 khelper
   14 root      20   0     0    0    0 S  0.0  0.0  0:00.00 kdevtmpfs
   15 root       0 -20     0    0    0 S  0.0  0.0  0:00.00 netns
```

top showing resource contention

It looks like a MySQL server is also running on this node and is taking up a lot of system memory. We suspect that resource contention with MySQL is probably what's causing the operating system to kill Elasticsearch. We are able to move the MySQL database to its own dedicated host, and after a few weeks with no more memory issues, we can conclude that this resolved the problem.

# Query requests slow and timing out

Users of our corporate Elasticsearch-backed web application have started reporting that the search functionality is slow and sometimes doesn't return at all. We are able to verify this by running a few searches on the web application, and we decide to use Kopf to investigate the issue. In Kopf, we notice that the disk indicator is red for one of our nodes, elasticsearch-node-01, as seen in the following screenshot:

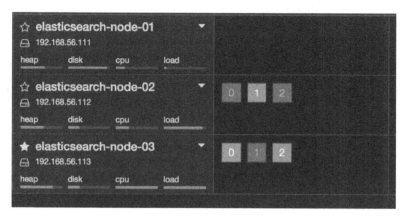

Kopf shows that elasticsearch-node-01 is low on disk space

The red **disk** indicator for elasticsearch-node-01 means that we are low on disk space. Also, all of the node's shards have been reallocated to other nodes. Checking the log of elasticsearch-node-01 at /var/log/elasticsearch/my_elasticsearch_cluster.log, we confirm that the disk is full by seeing the **no space left on device** message. We are able to resolve the issue by adding an additional hard drive to all nodes in the cluster and configuring Elasticsearch to use the new space in the elasticsearch.yml file.

To prevent this issue in the future, we decide to install Nagios using the instructions found in *Chapter 5, System Monitoring*, in order to send out e-mail alerts the next time the disk space gets low.

# Summary

This chapter looked into how to diagnose node failures, determine the root cause of the problem, and apply corrective action. Some key things we learned are:

- Many errors, from shard failures to slow query performance, are caused by `OutOfMemoryError` exceptions

- Running out of disk space on one node can cause other nodes to run out of disk space as well when shards are reallocated

- Running Elasticsearch alongside other services that require a lot of memory can result in the operating system killing Elasticsearch to free up memory

The next chapter will talk about Elasticsearch 5.0, the next major release of the platform, and it will give you an overview of the various new monitoring tools that will accompany the Elasticsearch 5.0 release.

# 8
# Looking Forward

This final chapter discusses the next major release of Elasticsearch, version 5.0, which is a significant upgrade over 2.3.2. It introduces a number of API enhancements, in addition to several performance and reliability updates. Many of these changes will, for better or for worse, affect your interaction with and monitoring of an Elasticsearch cluster.

The specific topics we'll discuss in this chapter include:

- Elasticsearch 5 overview
- Upgrading to Elasticsearch 5
- Monitoring Elasticsearch 5

## Elasticsearch 5 overview

Elasticsearch 5 will follow Elasticsearch 2 as the next major software release. Although this may be chronologically jarring, Elastic.co purposefully jumped from version 2 to 5 to better synchronize the updated version of Elasticsearch with several other Elastic.co products, including Kibana, Logstash, Marvel (called **Monitoring** in 5.0), and more. This update will help ensure that all Elastic.co software running on a cluster is both compatible and up-to-date.

There are hundreds of new changes being introduced in version 5, but a few relevant highlights include:

- Compatibility between the Elasticsearch 2 API and Elasticsearch 5
- Indices from Elasticsearch 2 can be migrated to version 5:
    - Indices from Elasticsearch 1 must first be migrated to version 2 before migrating them to version 5

- Marvel is renamed Monitoring
- The Elasticsearch-Logstash-Kibana stack is renamed the **Elastic Stack**
- The plugin API no longer supports site plugins, including plugins such as Elasticsearch-head, Bigdesk, and Kopf
- The warmers API is removed in favor of eager field data loading and disk-based norms
- Lucene version upgraded from 5 to 6
- Several configuration changes, including removal of all system environment variables, such as `ES_HEAP`, in favor of Java VM command-line arguments
- `text` and `keyword` mapping types deprecated in favor of `string` type
- `bin/plugin` renamed to `bin/elasticsearch-plugin`

> Elasticsearch-head, Bigdesk, and Kopf have not yet been updated to be compatible with Elasticsearch 5. When they are upgraded, they will run as standalone applications, similar to Kibana.

# Performance and reliability

Elasticsearch 5 introduces several performance and reliability improvements, including:

- Indexing performance improved 15-20% for small documents
- Lucene 6 improves search time by 25% and decreases disk space usage by 50% for numeric, date, and geospatial fields
- The `elasticsearch.yml` settings file is now strictly validated, meaning Elasticsearch won't start if there is a configuration error
- If a production node (meaning a node that isn't bound to the `localhost` address) doesn't have enough file handles available, or doesn't have permission to lock the system's memory usage via the `mlockall` setting, it will throw an exception and won't start

# Data loss

Elasticsearch 2 has a well-publicized, ongoing issue in which, in rare circumstances involving networking problems and a network partition, Elasticsearch can drop data during ingestion.

Writes made to Elasticsearch during the network partition will be confirmed, but not all will actually make it to the index. The Elasticsearch team has made a strong effort to address this problem, and many—but not all—instances of the bug are fixed in the new version. In consideration of this, contemplate the following when building an Elasticsearch-backed application in both version 2 and version 5:

- Don't use Elasticsearch as a primary data store. Instead, use a database such as HBase, Cassandra, PostgreSQL, or another, depending on your data size and requirements.

- Be sure to verify that the number of data records in your primary data store match those in Elasticsearch.

- Have a plan to re-index data in the event of data loss.

While data loss is *very* unlikely, the potential impact is huge and it is important to have a plan of action in place.

# Upgrading to Elasticsearch 5.0

Elasticsearch 5 version will be released soon. It's a good idea to start testing your cluster's compatibility with the new version. To help with the upgrade process, Elastic.co offers a tool called the **Elasticsearch Migration Helper**. Install this tool as an Elasticsearch 2.3 plugin:

```
sudo /usr/share/elasticsearch/bin/plugin install
  https://github.com/elastic/
  elasticsearch-migration/releases/download/v2.0-alpha2/
  elasticsearch-migration-2.0-alpha2.zip
```

 The Elasticsearch Migration Helper is only compatible with Elasticsearch 2.3.

After installing the plugin, open it in the browser by visiting `http://elasticsearch-node-01:9200/_plugin/elasticsearch-migration/`, as seen in the following screenshot:

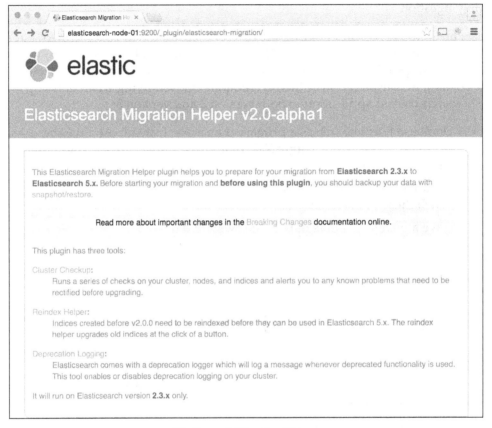

Elasticsearch Migration Helper

The **Cluster Checkup** diagnostic will display a report of the necessary updates before using Elasticsearch 5:

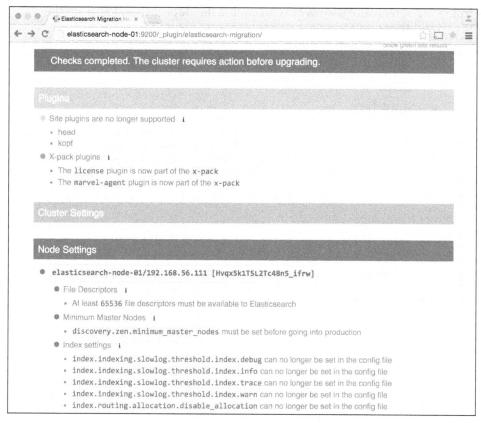

Elasticsearch Migration Helper configuration check report

The **Cluster Checkup** shows us that we'll have to remove some incompatible plugins before moving to Elasticsearch 5, including Elasticsearch-head, Kopf, and the Marvel Agent. We'll also have to update a few system and node configuration settings before upgrading.

After fixing all of these configuration issues, we can use the Elasticsearch Migration Helper to enable the deprecation log. This log file records anytime we call an Elasticsearch API method that will be deprecated or removed in version 5.

The following screenshot shows how to enable the deprecation log from the Elasticsearch Migration Helper:

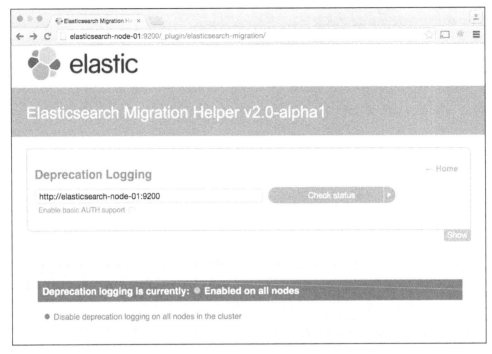

Click the Enable/Disable link to activate the deprecation log

Once the log is enabled, it can be found at:

```
/var/log/elasticsearch/<cluster_name>_deprecation.log
```

# When to upgrade

After running the Elasticsearch Migration Helper and correcting all relevant errors and warnings, it's safe to upgrade to Elasticsearch 5 in a development environment. You can now test the application to ensure that everything works with the new version. Pay close attention to the deprecation log and note things that you'll need to fix.

Since this is such a major release, it may be worth delaying your production upgrade until a few months after the General Availability release. As with any new piece of software, there may be bugs with early versions of Elasticsearch 5 that will be fixed shortly after it is made generally available.

# Monitoring Elasticsearch 5

Elastic.co rebranded its suite of monitoring tools, including the Elasticsearch-Logstash-Kibana (ELK) stack, in Elasticsearch 5. Marvel is now renamed **Monitoring** and comes bundled with some additional monitoring tools. The ELK stack is now just the **Elastic Stack**.

The Elasticsearch X-Pack is a premium suite of monitoring tools that Elastic.co charges an annual fee for running in production. The X-Pack consists of the following tools:

- **Monitoring**: Previously Marvel

- **Shield**: Adds authentication, access control, and HTTPS support to Elasticsearch

- **Watcher**: Similar to Nagios, but with some Elasticsearch-specific features, such as sending email alerts if a query runs slow

- **Graph**: Network-graph data visualization tool

- **Reporting**: Generates PDF reports based on data in Kibana

Kibana and Marvel also received an updated look and feel, as seen in the following screenshots:

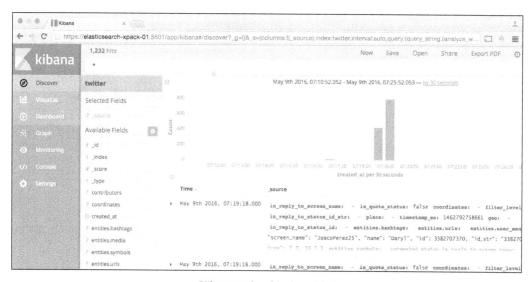

Kibana updated look and feel

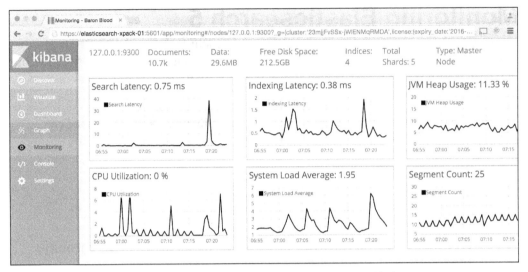

Marvel is now Monitoring with an updated look and feel

# Summary

This chapter examined the upcoming Elasticsearch 5 release, discussed upgrading to version 5, and touched on the new monitoring tools available in the Elasticsearch X-Pack. Some takeaways from this chapter include:

- Elasticsearch 5 has some big performance and reliability gains, but also some breaking changes to the API.

- Elasticsearch-head, Bigdesk, and Kopf are not yet compatible with Elasticsearch 5.

- Elasticsearch 5 is a major release, and upgrading from version 2 may not be a simple process. Be sure to run the Elasticsearch Migration Helper before upgrading.

- The Elasticsearch X-Pack provides a suite of monitoring tools for Elasticsearch 5, but isn't free.

Thanks for reading *Monitoring Elasticsearch*. I hope you learned some new techniques for monitoring and troubleshooting an Elasticsearch cluster. If you take only one thing away from reading this book, I hope it is to be meticulous and to test at every step of the way when troubleshooting issues that pop up when working with Elasticsearch.

If you feel like giving back to the Elasticsearch community, please consider making contributions to the Elasticsearch-head, Bigdesk, or Kopf projects. These are all excellent open source tools that make the lives of everyone working with Elasticsearch easier. And, as mentioned in this chapter, they all need to be re-architected and updated to work with Elasticsearch 5.

> You can read more about the following topics here:
> - Elasticsearch-head: `https://github.com/mobz/elasticsearch-head`
> - Bigdesk: `https://github.com/lukas-vlcek/bigdesk`
> - Kopf: `https://github.com/lmenezes/elasticsearch-kopf`

Also, feel free to reach out to me on Twitter: `@dwnoble`.

# Index

## A

**Apache Lucene**
  reference link 7
**Atomicity, Consistency, Isolation,**
    **and Durability (ACID) 7**

## B

**Bigdesk**
  about 29, 42-45
  installing 23
  reference 45
**bulk indexing operations 122, 123**

## C

**case studies, node failures**
  ES process, terminating 144
  queries, timing out 145
  slow queries requests 145
**cluster**
  about 21
  Bigdesk, installing 23, 24
  Elasticsearch-head, installing 21, 22
  Marvel 24
  Marvel Dashboard, installing 25
**Cluster API**
  reference 46
**cluster management tools, more dropdown**
  Aliases 79
  Analysis 79
  Cat APIs 79
  Cluster Settings 79
  Create Index 79
  Hot Threads 79

Index Templates 79
Percolator 79
Snapshot 79
Warmers 79
**cold indices 111-114**
**command line tools, for system and process**
    **management**
  about 97
  df command 101, 102
  du command 101, 102
  free command 101
  grep command 98
  kill command 100
  ps command 99
  tail command 98
  top command 97

## D

**data ingestion**
  bulk indexing operations 122, 123
  drive configuration 124
  optimizing 121, 122
**disk size**
  _source field, storing 120, 121
  analyzed field, storing 120, 121
  compression level, increasing 119
  reducing 119
**disk space**
  about 142
  issue, resolving 143
**drive configuration 124**

## E

**eager field data**
  URL 115

**Elasticsearch**
  about 1
  data distribution 2-5
  fault tolerance 2-5
  full-text search 5-7
  installing 12
  monitoring 8, 9
  open source full-text search engines 7
  overview 1
  process crashes 141, 142
  redundancy 2-5
  reference link 12
  version, reference link 12
**Elasticsearch 5**
  data loss 149
  monitoring 153
  overview 147, 148
  performance and reliability
      improvements 148
  upgrading 149-152
  upgrading, situation 152
**Elasticsearch cat API**
  about 29, 46
  background 46
  document count 47
  health color code 47
  indices 48
  reference 46
  shards 49
**Elasticsearch cluster configuration**
  about 16
  cluster name 16
  max file descriptors, updating on Ubuntu
      Linux 18
  maximum files limit 18
  memory configuration 17
  open files limit 17
  open files limit, verifying 19
  pluggable authentication modules,
      enabling 19
  swapping, disabling 20, 21
**Elasticsearch-head**
  about 29, 33
  Any Request tab 41
  Browser tab 40
  cluster states 34-37
  Indices tab 39

  installing 21
  node and index actions 37-39
  Overview tab 33, 34
  reference, for official website 42
  Structured Query tab 40
**Elasticsearch installation**
  CentOS/RHEL 14
  configuration files 16
  DEB/RPM installation 13
  reference link 13
  Ubuntu/Debian, using 13
  verification 14, 15
  yum 14
  yum and apt-get repositories, using 13
**Elasticsearch, Logstash, and Kibana (ELK)**
  about 73, 80
  uses 80
**Elasticsearch Mappings**
  reference link 7
**Elasticsearch Migration Helper 149**
**Elasticsearch Search API**
  reference link 7
**elasticsearch.yml configuration options**
  marvel.agent.cluster.state.timeout 59
  marvel.agent.cluster.stats.timeout 59
  marvel.agent.indices 59
  marvel.agent.interval 59
  marvel.enabled 59
  marvel.history.duration 59
**Elastic Stack 148, 153**

# F

**features, Elasticsearch**
  analytics 2
  distributed 2
  Dynamic Mappings 2
  fault tolerant 2
  full-text search 2
  JSON document store 2
  non-relational 2
  NoSQL 2
**fielddata cache**
  about 106
  size, limiting 106
  verifying 106, 107

## H

hot nodes 118
Hot-Warm architecture
  about 118
  hot nodes 118
  master nodes 118
  URL 119
  warm nodes 118, 119
human readable (-h flag) 102

## I

Indices API
  reference 46
installations
  about 80
  Kibana 84
  Kopf 74-76
  Logstash 81

## J

Java Runtime Environment (JRE) 11

## K

Kibana
  download link 84
  installing 84-91
  working with 80
Kopf
  about 73
  installing 74-78
  working with 73
Kopf installation
  cluster page 76
  more dropdown 79
  nodes page 77
  REST page 78

## L

Logstash
  configuration file, reference link 83
  installing 81
  working with 80

## M

Marvel
  about 24, 25, 51
  agent configuration settings 58, 59
  components 24
  configuring 57
  dashboard 61
  index configuration 59, 60
  setting up 51-56
  upgrading 56, 57
Marvel dashboard
  about 61, 62
  Indices dashboard 66-69
  Nodes dashboard 69-71
  Overview dashboard 63-65
master nodes 118
Monitoring 147

## N

Nagios
  check script for Elasticsearch, reference
    link 92
  installing 92-97
  working with 92
Nagios Remote Plugin Executor (NRPE) 92
NGINX logs
  loading 81-83
node configuration
  case study 124, 125
node failures
  case studies 143
  disk space 142
  Elasticsearch process crashes 141, 142
  monitoring 71, 72
  OutOfMemoryError exceptions 132
  problems, diagnosing 131, 132

## O

open source full-text search engines
  Apache Lucene 7
  Ferret 8
  Solr 8
OutOfMemoryError exceptions
  about 132
  resolving 138-140

shard failures 133-137
slow queries 137, 138

## P

**problem solving**
themes 9

## Q

**queries**
analyzing 108
slow log 108, 109
**query optimization**
case study 126-129
**query performance**
cold indices 111-114
high-cardinality fields 110
improving 110
script queries 117
shard query cache 115-117
smaller indices, querying 110, 111
testing, meticulously 117, 118

## R

**RAID 0 124**
**Red Hat Enterprise Linux (RHEL) 11**

## S

**script queries 117**
**Search API query 78**
**shard failures**
about 133
example 133-137
**shard query cache**
about 115-117
URL 117
**shards 3**

**slow queries**
about 137
example 137, 138
**states, Elasticsearch-head**
green 34
red 34
yellow 34
**stream2es utility**
reference link 31
**system configuration 105, 106**
**system performance**
improving 118

## T

**three-node Elasticsearch cluster**
configuring 30
sample data 31-33
setting up 29

## U

**Ubuntu Linux**
max file descriptors, updating 18

## W

**warmers**
reference link 115
**warm nodes 118, 119**
**web application optimization**
case study 130

## X

**X-Pack, tools**
graph 153
monitoring 153
reporting 153
shield 153
watcher 153

www.ingramcontent.com/pod-product-compliance
Lightning Source LLC
Chambersburg PA
CBHW060135060326
40690CB00018B/3881